And Always
One More Time

And Always One More Time

A Memoir

Margaret Mandell

atmosphere press

In Memoriam
Herbert Elliot Mandell, M.D.
Who taught me to love unconditionally.

Dedicated to
John Crothers Pollock III, Ph.D.
Who loved me back to life.

Contents

Prologue

My Dearest Love, Herb:

I am swimming laps alone in my brother's infinity pool in Kiawah, South Carolina. Alligators sun themselves on the golf course by the muddy moat three feet below the pool, next to a sign: "Beware of Alligators." You are inside the house. *When will you come outside and join me?* I think.

We used to swim side by side across Sengekontacket Pond. A mile wide, and I never let you out of my sight. Before the wracking cough started.

Suddenly, you appear by the edge of the pool, all six feet of you, chiseled, long-limbed, and lean. I pause, dripping, grasping the ladder directly below you, squinting into the sun at your handsome silhouette.

"I know what I have," you say. "I've been researching my symptoms all morning on the Internet. It's worse than cancer. There is no treatment, no cure. Pulmonary fibrosis is fatal. In a few months, my lungs will turn to Velcro. I will suffocate."

You turn and walk away.

I resume swimming laps. I want nothing more in that moment than to forget what you just said. I hate that you are always right. Especially now.

In medical school, years before you became a psychiatrist, you came home one day and said to me, "Today, our teacher told us all we needed to know:

'Listen to the patient—nine times out of ten, you've got the diagnosis right there.'"

My Dearest Love, Herb:

You loved her. I loved her. Before your cough, we both loved yoga with Maryann. Like you, she had large, empathic brown eyes and a smile that radiated *you're the only person in the room.*

You could tell she was a dancer. She floated in and out of poses like a ballerina. She would sashay into Studio A, the one with the mirrors on three walls, and exclaim while clutching her coffee, "Wow! Twelve people at 6 a.m.!" Men, including you, were attracted to her full-figured body and cherubic face framed by a halo of thick black curls.

"Find your e-e-e-e-edge," she intoned. "*There* it is!" You loved it when Maryann said, "Thank yourself for taking care of your body. Thank your body for taking care of you. Namaste."

She affirmed all your hard work to stay healthy—eating well, working out, zero body fat—a point of pride with you. Remember in college how your best friend called you "my-body-is-a-temple-Herb"? Most of all, you were lured by the sound of Maryann's voice, full-throated and hypnotic.

We all were.

Three months after our trip to Kiawah, you sat at our kitchen table, forehead creased in thought, your body wracked with pneumonia, the end of the road for anyone with pulmonary fibrosis. Out of the blue, between coughs, you said hoarsely, "Thank myself for taking care of my body? I think I could have taken better care of my body. I was such a workaholic."

Yes, my love, you were.

My Dearest Love, Herb:

Do you remember what you said at dinner that night after you were too sick to leave the house?

"This is not what you signed up for," you said.

You're dying, and you're thinking of me? I thought.

"This is our love story," I said. "There is no place else I'd rather be."

"What do you want for your birthday?" you asked.

"The only thing I want I cannot have," I said.

My Dearest Love, Herb:

Our last hug.

We stood in the kitchen by the fridge, your lungs already at twenty-five-percent capacity. By then, you panted all the time. I held you close, smelled your Old Spice deodorant, and felt your long, still-strong arms around me and the straining muscles in your chest. I listened to your rapid inhalations and exhalations, breath shallow and struggling.

"I am really dying," you whispered, lungs crackling like Jiffy Pop in the microwave. *Pop, pop, pop.*

"But you are here right this minute," I said, drinking you in, holding on for dear life as if I were the one who had to leave. The fridge hummed.

My Dearest Love, Herb:

In the hospital, you could no longer speak, and yet you had so much to say.

"I tried to be a good provider," you said hoarsely just before they covered your mouth and nose with the oxygen mask. I nodded, swallowing hard. I could see you were suffocating, struggling to speak. You gestured for pen and paper, right hand writing in the air.

"No Temple!" you scribbled frantically in all capital letters on the legal pad I gave you, terrified they were going to ship you out of Abington and back to Temple University Hospital, where you were undergoing evaluation for a lung transplant.

"No Temple!" I said, smoothing your crumpled sheets. You told us the day before in the ER you wanted to die right there in Abington Hospital, where you had your first job out of residency and where our daughter was born.

"Left foot itches," you scribbled on the pad.

I watched your face through the oxygen mask as I scratched the sole of your left foot, wondering how I would know when the itching had stopped.

I'd massaged your feet night after night with those lavender-scented Ayurvedic creams after your knee replacement.

"It feels so good," you always said.

This time, you gave no signal.

A few hours later, at 9:30 p.m., your breathing slowed and stopped. Your jaw shuddered and then was still. As your heart monitor flatlined, I kept whispering into your ear, "Thank you, thank you, thank you, thank you," thinking if I said it enough times, you would hear me. Your ear was still warm against my lips.

It was Tuesday.

First, I called the kids, who an hour before had kissed you goodnight and left, expecting to see you the next day. Lydia, already back in Center City, erupted into explosive sobs. I could see her small frame doubled over, convulsed in agony. *Daddy.*

Dan, who had been about to go to bed in our house after staying up the previous night by your side, took an Uber back to the hospital as soon as I called. He dragged over the blue Naugahyde chair and sat by your right shoulder, gazing at your gaunt, ashen face. He turned to me and said, "Dad looked death right in the eye."

Next, I called Rabbi Josh, who had already prayed at your bedside earlier in the day when you could no longer open your eyes. I still imagined then that you could hear his comforting words over the grinding *whoosh* of the BiPAP machine forcing air into your spastic lungs. Now, his voice comforted me as I was pleading over the phone: "Could we please, please have Herb's funeral at the synagogue?"

I went home and crawled into your side of the bed.

Friday, at your synagogue funeral, I clung to our children and stared at the floor.

Friday night, a blizzard dumped twenty-two inches of snow on Philadelphia.

Saturday, we shoveled the front walk without you.

My Dearest Love, Herb:

I yelled at the flowers. The ones that you sent on your deathbed. You were still texting after you could not speak and managed to have flowers delivered for my birthday.

"Let us make the most of the time we have left," you had the florist write on the card. The flowers outlive you by a week.

The day after you died, I sit by your empty seat at the kitchen table, struggling to write your obituary for the *Jewish Exponent*. Cheerful yellow and white blossoms at my elbow fill the stale indoor air with sweet perfume. I cannot imagine reducing your beautiful life to a lifeless list of diplomas and titles.

Herbert E. Mandell, M.D., November 12, 1949–January 19, 2016

Dr. Mandell served as Fellow of the American Psychiatric Association as well as President of the Regional Council of Child and Adolescent Psychiatry and was Clinical Assistant Professor of Child and Adolescent Psychiatry at Temple University School of Medicine. A graduate of Thomas Jefferson University School of Medicine and the Institute of the Psychoanalytic Center of Philadelphia, Dr. Mandell worked evenings and weekends in private practice while concurrently holding Clinical and Medical Director positions at five area hospitals. He is survived by his wife, two adult children, and a brother.

This is not you. All I want, then and now, is to see the light in your eyes.

Suddenly, I yell, "Why are these goddamn flowers still here and you're not?"

My Dearest Love, Herb:

It's been eleven months since you died. I am still afraid to open the small wooden box filled with your ashes. Night after night, your box stares at me from across the room as I lay on your side of the bed, hoping to catch a scent of you from your pillow. Finally, this morning, I sit bolt upright and eye the box, swing my legs over the side of the bed, and tiptoe towards the bureau. I want to hold you.

I approach the box and open it. I lift the ten-pound bag of your remains and cup you tenderly against my heart. You feel and sound crunchy, like a bean bag. Your smell is gone.

"I forgive you," I whisper to your ashes, "I forgive you for leaving me," not realizing until I held you just then how furious I was. But then I remember yelling at the flowers the day after you died.

I give your Ziplock bag one last tender caress and whisper a prayer of thanks for all that you were, all 162 pounds of you, *once so much more than this.* Gently placing your remains back in the box and closing the lid, I stroke the simple brass plate that bears your name.

Herbert Elliot Mandell. Nineteen letters. Ten pounds of ash. A paragraph for the newspaper. The one who, on his deathbed, sent flowers for my birthday.

My Dearest Love, Herb:

Within a year after you died, I'd given away or sold all your stuff. Your clothes (I kept the yellow sweater that I loved), barbells, pellet gun for scaring away the geese, forty-two neckties, the complete works of Sigmund Freud, never-opened *Encyclopedia Britannica*, and bicycle.

But I still miss, like a phantom limb, your bright red Kipling backpack that traveled back and forth with you every day to your Abington Club workouts. Inside the backpack were a stick of Old Spice deodorant, a hairbrush full of your curly white hair, and clean underwear. When it was not on your back, it hung cheerfully on the metal handle of the casement window at the foot of the back staircase next to our kitchen door, always at the ready for the next workout and the next and the next, until, too sick to breathe, let alone pedal a stationary bike, you stopped leaving the house.

On Sunday, January 17, you said, "Take me to the ER."

You never came home. Still, I believed you might if the red backpack remained there. For months, it hung from the window handle. At the ready. I knew what was inside without opening it. Preparing to move, even after I emptied our house around it, I was unable to touch, open, or move the red backpack. Each day, it called to me as I walked by. "You know what you have to do," it taunted. One night, I grabbed the straps and hurled it into the trash can just outside the kitchen door, slamming down the lid. Trash night! And before I could change my mind, I sprinted up the driveway to the street, dragging the can.

My Dearest Love, Herb:

On a bright, cold day exactly one year after your death, the kids and I met out back in the gazebo overlooking the pond, your happy place. I carried the Ziplock bag with your ashes and, using a stainless-steel coffee scoop, took the first spoonful and threw you over the side of the gazebo.

A gust of wind came out of nowhere and pulled you up towards the sky. We watched the sun sparkling on your crystal filaments—angel dust, you. Then, slowly, the air grew still, and you landed in the frozen grass. Lydia formed you into the shape of a heart under the dogwood tree you planted by the pond. Dan poured you in a circle around the roots of the white pine tree he started as a tiny sprout in fifth grade, now taller than the house. We went to the grotto, and Lydia sprinkled you inside that magical quartz cave you loved so much. Dan tossed you into the exact spot where you pulled him out of the pond when he fell in at age four. In the woods, he re-enacted his little boy's fears of the dark along the wood chip path, walking in, walking out, walking back in a little further.

"Thank you, Dad, for taking away my fear, for making it safe," he said between sobs.

I climbed into the fishing twine hammock strung between two trees above the dam and rocked there a bit, hugging you in your Ziplock bag, remembering the Nova Scotia fisherman we met, who tied all the knots by hand. I threw a scoop of you down the little waterfall towards the pond next door. Into the woods, we scattered you amongst beloved buried pets whose graves you solemnly dug: Dusty the chinchilla, Mo the ferret, Henry Chanukah Hamster, and countless bunnies. Dan took you to the perimeter of our property, demarcating the "fiefdom" you tended so carefully. Lydia led us out front and placed the last of your ashes right under the mailbox.

"This is your home," she said, "you lived here." She had the three of us hold hands by the pachysandra. We each had the fine white powder of your ashes covering our hands, clothing, and shoes.

"I have Dad all over me," Lydia said, looking down at her blue jeans, now chalky white.

As the kids and I walked slowly back into the house with your empty Ziplock bag, I clung to them both, as I did during your funeral. But this time, I felt lighter.

How does it feel to be spread over two acres? And all over your wife and children?

A Detour Around My Belly Button

The first anniversary of Herb's death looms, as well as memories of our final weeks together. How we scrambled each day through the maze of Temple University Hospital as he underwent invasive procedures to determine his eligibility for a lung transplant. Stalwart, he was uncomplaining. Fasting, drinking chalky dyes. Cardiac catheterization. Endless blood draws. He would die before he became eligible.

I am walking around the Michener Museum in Doylestown with a friend as a nagging pain grows in my belly. When we leave to head to a chic French restaurant, I barely notice the colorful Christmas lights chasing away the December gloom as the pain worsens. At the restaurant, I order sea bass, broccoli rabe, and smashed garlic potatoes, which I will see again four hours later in an emesis basin as I lie on a gurney writhing in pain at the Abington Hospital ER.

How I manage to drive myself home all the way from Doylestown on the Pennsylvania Turnpike, I do not know. How I finally call the ambulance from my bedroom at home while I still can speak, I do not know. How I remember to grab my phone and charger and keys and insurance cards as I collapse on the stretcher outside my kitchen door, I do not know. Here's what I do know: I just saved my own life without my doctor husband around to look after me. *So, this is what the inside of an ambulance looks like.* I am shivering, teeth chattering. At the

ER, my gurney rushes through the same threshold I watched Herb cross for the last time.

I answer the same questions over and over:

"The pain started at four p.m. I had dinner at six p.m." It is nearly midnight.

When the male nurse asks, "What did you eat?" I projectile-vomit the entire dinner, undigested, into a basin.

Pausing to notice the bright green color of the broccoli rabe, I reply, "Here it is!" He is not amused.

After X-rays, a CT-scan requiring ingestion of thirty-two ounces of dye, and more vomiting up the dye flecked with broccoli rabe, I am rushed to the OR, morphine coursing through my veins. "Bring her up here *immediately*," the surgeon barks into the phone.

"Cecal volvulus," he tells me upon arrival. "Your twisted bowel is about to burst, and if it does, there will be sepsis and likely death."

No, I think, *my children cannot be orphaned twice in one year.*

At 2 a.m., I sign the consent form as the surgeon, the cheerful Dr. Ryan Shadis, leans over my gurney. I have just agreed to a possible colostomy.

"Do you have any idea what time it is?" I ask him, punch-drunk on morphine. "*It's the middle of the night!*"

"That's why they pay me the big bucks," Shadis replies affably. Anesthesiologists chuckle. I hoist my distended body from the gurney onto the cold, hard metal operating table, surprised by how narrow it is, and think, *I could fall off either side.* I am shivering hard, naked. A nurse puts socks on my feet. Everyone is wearing shower caps. The lights are blinding.

I awaken two hours later in recovery, minus two feet of bowel, with a train track of fourteen staples running from above my navel, around my belly button, like a detour, all the way down to my pubic hair, which has been shaved. There is a nasogastric tube up my nose, running down my throat and into my stomach, pumping bile continuously into a bag hanging beside me; a catheter is in my bladder with its very own bag. I am retching from the anesthesia, which tugs on the staples. The dry heaving will last for three days, and I will beg for water, beg for the tube down my throat to be removed. "Can't risk it," they would say. "Your intestines are in shock. You need to get up and walk around, help your body expel the anesthesia." *Walk around?*

I am ruined, I think, the next morning in the hospital bathroom as, dragging my IV pole, I lift my hospital gown and look in the mirror at my emaciated torso, ribs protruding, in the harsh fluorescent lights, and at the foot-long gash in my bloody, stapled abdomen. I had already decided when Herb died that no one would ever want this sixty-something leftover body again. Now, I am certain. Suddenly, a cascade of bloody shit erupts from my colon onto the bathroom floor. I squat to wipe it up. Strong yoga legs! *No way I'm leaving this for a nurse to clean up. Mom would be proud.*

Later that day, I wonder aloud to my son Dan on the phone: "How did my surgeon, Ryan Shadis, even know what to do? How many people had to die of a twisted bowel before the 'right hemi-colectomy' was perfected?" To which Dan, ever the scientist, replies, "We all stand on the shoulders of giants."

Back home after the surgery, I am too weak from blood loss to stand at the stove, so Cousin Ellen comes to cook for me, arriving with a cooler full of beef bone broth, beets, pastured eggs, salmon roe, leafy greens, and other iron-rich foods from her farm.

"Oh my God," she gasps one night in the middle of dinner, "in ancient Chinese medicine, the colon is the organ of grief and letting go!" We put down our forks and let it sink in. I imagine my colon twisting and writhing as the first anniversary of Herb's death approaches.

"And lungs are the seat of sadness," I say after a few moments, remembering Herb weeping inconsolably through the untimely deaths of his older brother and younger sister, each from stage four cancer, shortly before his poor lungs turned to Velcro.

For us both, and maybe for everyone, the issue was in the tissue.

One Yoga Pose at a Time

Exactly two years since Herb died.

What am I doing here—back at the Kripalu Yoga Center in western Massachusetts, where Herb and I once went together and shared a double room with two narrow cots, one sink, and a bathroom down the hall? This time, I sleep beside a randomly assigned roommate, Beth, who hates that the bathroom is down the hall.

It is 6:30 a.m., still pre-dawn. I sit on the floor, with blocks and straps on a mat I wish were thicker. It's morning meditation, and already, my arthritic back is starting to throb. The day wears on as we students are paired up to practice-teach poses to one another, mindful of "ground-up" cues in front of watchful teachers. Oy, shoulder stand. Why can't I get my butt off the floor?

"Bring your elbows in, closer to your body," says a teacher called Yoganand.

I can't, I think, arms shaking. My partners are so much younger than I am.

All day long, we are critiqued and assessed.

6 p.m. Dark again. We break for dinner with hours of homework to do.

Kripalu Yoga Teacher Training: two-hundred hours, twenty-four days.

I thought I was training to teach postures. But we are tested on anatomy, physiology, philosophy, and Sanskrit. This is more than I bargained for. It is dawning on me, as I struggle on the yoga mat and dare to become a teacher, how yoga *is the practice of tolerating the consequences of being yourself.*

Who will I be without Herb?

*

Home for the holidays, I drag my roller bag from the airport train up the hill to our empty house in the dark. The wheels of my roller bag bump over tree roots in our driveway. Christmas lights twinkle next door against the black sky. I look for Herb in the kitchen and imagine him waiting for me at the door. But the house is dark. He isn't asking me what's for dinner. He isn't here to help with anatomy. He isn't here, calling me Mouse, asking me to teach a class, insisting I am a natural.

He isn't here.

*

The next day at the movies, I stuff my face with popcorn. I leave battered with a tummy ache, throbbing teeth, and cuts on my tongue. I leave, still, as the person I have always been—an overeater who, as a young child, wanted what my four younger brothers had: their Halloween candy, their Easter baskets, and, before that, their baby food. Mashed bananas were my favorite.

I remember sitting, as a ten-year-old, finishing dinner at the square Formica table in our small breakfast room with red-and-yellow vinyl-covered benches. Dad is ranting about his latest altercation at work, crunching loudly on mustard pickles, dipping them into the yellow brine. Mom is smoking, red lipstick stains on the filter of her Marlborough, bored eyes half closed as she puffs and peels off chipped nail polish onto her plate. Five-year-old Andy is sullen. He is not allowed to leave the table until he finishes his brisket. I reach across him without asking and stick my fork into the congealed meat on his plate. He doesn't want it. Neither, really, do I. I eat it anyway.

Why, always, this hunger?

Here I sit in this empty house in the dead of winter. Holiday cards from absent dear ones lining the kitchen table. *Thank you for thinking of me.* One card, in particular, takes my breath away: Chanukah wishes from our Prince Edward Island landlords with a photo of our PEI cottage at sunrise. Suddenly, I am there, running outside at dawn to catch the shimmering first light over Fortune Bay, sprinting across the wet grass past the just opening daylilies by the steps, lobster boats already leaving from the wharf. Back inside, I whip up muffins from the blueberries we picked the day before, belly down on the kitchen floor to light the pilot in our ancient gas oven. Herb awakens to the smell of warm muffins and fresh coffee, tuning our small portable radio to CBC for the latest local news in the Canadian Maritimes, the weather report off nearby Nova Scotia always being reliable here in Eastern PEI. Soon, there would be the annual oyster shucking contest and the Rollo Bay Fiddle Festival across from the potato fields, musicians in campers pouring in from all over Canada. At breakfast, Herb maps out our bike ride for the morning: our favorite, a windy trek up to the East Point Lighthouse flanked by crashing surf and scrubby pines.

"Teach me some yoga," Herb says after lunch, back in our tiny cottage, barely enough room on the planked wood floor for two yoga mats, summer light pouring in from all sides, twinkling on Fortune Bay.

For a split second, gazing at the photo, I think I see his face peering out of the cottage window.

*

I am trying not to dread my sixty-seventh birthday this week. It coincides, as it always will, with the anniversary of Herb's death. I remember his last words in the hospital:

"Don't let me die on her birthday. Please don't let me die on her birthday," he begged, eyes fixed on the ICU ceiling tiles in supplication.

This year, I imagine he is taking me out on a date. I dress up in red to meet our kids for dinner, wearing the gold necklace and fancy coat he bought me. All I want is to see his face.

At the restaurant, at our table by a roaring fire, I glance up from my menu and gaze at our adult children while they joke and banter as always, re-enacting episodes from *The Simpsons*. Herb wouldn't have missed a beat. *The Simpsons* was the one show we watched together as a family, and Herb had always laughed the loudest and would be guffawing right now.

I search my children's animated features. Dan with his luminous brown eyes, high forehead, patrician nose, and winning smile. Lydia, with her doe-eyed, Madonna-shaped face, olive complexion, same high forehead, curly brown hair, and radiant smile.

Herb.

*

I have returned to Kripalu for the concluding two weeks of yoga teacher training a little less nervous, having practiced every day at home during the holiday hiatus to an audio file recorded at Kripalu by Yoganand. His real name is Michael Carroll, former dean of the Kripalu School of Yoga. "Feel how the breath opens your belly," he intoned through my laptop speaker, his voice like honey, "then feel the openness your breath brings to your entire body, opening your heart, opening your mind, opening you to life and *all that comes your way*."

I pictured him, lean and serene. Eyes as blue as robin's eggs. Translucent alabaster skin. We met on the very first day of yoga teacher training, and I felt his *presence*, as if his eyes were peering into my soul. Over break, the sound of his voice became my mystic resonance, a soothing companion in my empty home. For six weeks, I read and reread my *Anatomy of Movement* textbook in between practice sessions with Yoganand, working to integrate book learning with muscle memory. My doctor husband was gone, but I held him close as I pictured him poring over *Gray's Anatomy* in his frizzy 1970s mutton chops.

I wanted to understand yoga as a *physical* experience: what the body could do and how it did it was all based on anatomical architecture. The health benefits of the poses excited me—every pose *did* something good, just as every nutrient-dense food nourished. Chest openers benefitted the endocrine system and glands, such as the thymus gland, which made T-cells and supported immunity. Inversions, head below the heart, benefited the lymphatic system, lungs, diaphragm, and abdominal organs, in addition to stretching and strengthening posterior muscles, improving bone density, and activating the parasympathetic nervous system.

I return now to Kripalu enthralled by a miracle: how all the tissues of the body respond to movement and confer health. I am open to *all that comes my way.*

*

Each morning, I arise at 4:30, an hour before my classmates, to sit alone in the quiet Pine-Sol-scented cafeteria, writing to Herb, always a cup of steaming, raw-honey-sweetened Earl Gray tea at my elbow. I sniff the damp air from an open window I can't locate; snow is coming. I lose myself in page after page as I write, chronicling my yoga teacher training adventure for Herb. How can it be nearly 6:30 already? Again, I have lost track of the time. I scamper off to morning sadhana down the stairwell, past my favorite Maya Angelou poster: *Have enough courage to trust love one more time and always one more time.*

How, Maya, how do you do that?

Slowly, I am learning from Yoganand and my Kripalu teachers how to weave a spiritual practice as inquiry by returning to my theme like the refrain in a prayer:

"Can you let go of tension in the neck as you let go of a grudge?"

"Can you find forgiveness in your heart as you release your lower back?"

"Can you love your beautiful body as you feel compassion for another?"

Can you keep loving when the man you love is gone?

Two months ago, I doubted whether I could get through yoga teacher training. Now, about to graduate, I feel nostalgia for this once-Jesuit monastery built of brick and cinder block, nestled in the Berkshire Mountains, the building as austere as the people are warm.

Once, I was a school admissions director. Once, I was Herb's wife. I arrived here wondering, *who am I now?* What is my dharma, my purpose?

Perhaps, I think, I am a yoga teacher.

A yoga teacher with the flu.

For, on the very last day at Kripalu, graduation day, I woke up, my throat on fire. I grew sicker throughout the day as I traveled to Albany, feverish on the flight home. Teeth chattering as I boarded the small commuter plane, I thought of Herb, how Lydia and I wrapped his pneumonia-embattled body in four blankets for his final trip to the ER. Still, he shivered.

And here I am.

*

If Herb were here now, he'd be sixty-eight, aging alongside me with his artificial knees—the ones they said were guaranteed for fifteen years. He'd be sitting with me at the table doing taxes, complaining that the plumber charges too much, that we're putting the plumber's kids through college. He'd be hearing all about the wedding plans for Jake and Lydia.

But now, lying alone in the dark, I am starting to wonder, am I married to a ghost? Will I always be alone?

"Herb would want you to be happy," our chiropractor Ed said this week as he stretched out my hips. "Loneliness is a *disease*," he said. A disease? I never thought of it that way. What is the cure? Where do I go?

"First, you go out for coffee, and you always pay for yourself," said my brother Andy, encouraging me to try an online dating website.

"Herb would want you to find another man," sister-in-law Katie said on my first visit to Kiawah without Herb, alligators still there.

Then she turned to her husband, my brother Pete, and said, "If I die first, don't you even think about finding another woman."

In the dark of night, I take off Herb's ring and place it for safekeeping in that lopsided turquoise coil-pot Lydia made in preschool—the one I kept on my vanity all those years to hold my everyday jewelry.

I feel naked.

My Dearest Love, Herb:

You always left a big, expensive pink-and-purple card on my pillow the night before Valentine's Day. I've kept them all.

I danced for you last night as I practiced yoga alone in my living room. Daggers in my belly from bowel surgery long gone, replaced by the occasional tug in muscle where sutures once were. It's been over a year since my bowel twisted on itself, over two years since you died, and exactly two weeks since I became a certified yoga instructor.

My body surrendered to a spontaneous yoga flow—arms, legs, tailbone, fingertips, sternum, crown of head reaching in multiple directions, body standing tall, lengthening into full extension. It was in the flow, the transition between poses, that I found the dance. I imagined you watching as you once did when I danced around our bedroom, you lying there in bed and me hoping to arouse you, feeling your eyes on me. My worst fear: to be invisible. Yet, my body lives, taut muscles vibrating with pleasure at the memory of your dancing eyes.

Oh, to dance with you and for you just one more time. To receive one more card.

Oh, to have kissed you on your deathbed when I had the chance—our last night together in the ICU when you pursed your feverish, parched lips and I shook my head no, afraid of pneumonia germs. You turned your head away, disconsolate. You had just wished me a happy birthday, and I broke your heart. I can't rewrite that scene, no matter how many times I replay it. I can't get you back. Regret is a worm in my belly.

Dying, you said I would find someone else. I said *never*. Today, my third Valentine's Day alone, I took that first step, testing the waters of online dating.

"Silver Singles." A guy named John. Professor. Age seventy-five. From Princeton.

But I never got to kiss you good-bye.

John will want to kiss me on our second date. It will happen as we stand at The Plaza entrance after dinner and a movie, his face inclining towards mine until I feel the heat of his mouth, the tickle of his whiskers. He'll pucker up his full lips and crinkle his eyes but will not make those "come hither" kissy noises you always made—*smack, smack*—your lips so fine they could have been drawn in with a pencil.

I never got to kiss you good-bye.

Nineteen Again

After I upload my profile, I search for a recent photo that doesn't look sad. Hard to do since most of my happy photos are with Herb, most recently biking in Puglia. I am about to give up, but then I find one of me sitting astride my new Fuji bicycle in the Performance Cycle parking lot last spring, grinning with excitement: a new bike! I am wearing Herb's bright yellow crew neck sweater.

Once I pay the site's outrageous $350 fee, twenty matches appear in my inbox. I am hoping for a guy with silver hair, but bald would be okay. I examine each guy's picture, read what he wrote, and try to imagine being with him. So many guys upload out-of-focus selfies, headshots taken at a weird angle that exaggerate their nose hairs and nostrils. Their written answers are superficial and sparse, typo-strewn, like they don't care enough to proofread.

"Nope," I say nineteen times.

Then I see John, the college professor from Princeton, standing in snow on a mountain top somewhere out west. I zoom in on his happy smile, notice his outstretched arms, and imagine those arms wrapped around me. I like his thick, curly silver hair, the promise of "Silver Singles"!

He wrote:

I believe conversation is a window to the soul.

I love spending time with my sons and playing tennis with my buddies.

What makes me laugh? Life's inevitable humiliations.

My perfect day? Sunday morning on my deck with The New York Times, *eating avocado toast.*

I read it again. Something makes me wish I were the one who made that avocado toast.

I close my laptop, walk away, and look at myself in the mirror.

Time to pluck those white hairs out of my eyebrows again, I think. I wonder if this guy John would be interested in a sad widow who writes every morning to her deceased husband. I try to remember the joy I felt when Herb looked at me as if I were the only person in the room, brown eyes dancing.

I go back online, double-click on the mountaintop photo of John, and zoom in even closer. Is there a hint of sadness in *his* eyes—a story there? Perhaps he needs someone like me to make his eyes dance, too. *I'm going for John.*

"Happy Valentine's Day, John," I write, hitting the Silver Singles send-message button.

He answers right away: "Happy Valentine's Day! I just landed in Newark from a ski trip to Jackson Hole. More later."

Yes.

For the next several days, I open my laptop each morning, like unwrapping a present, hoping to find his latest message and compose my next carefully worded retort. *Keep it going!*

"I don't understand," he writes. "How is it that someone with a Ph.D. in history is a yoga instructor?"

"Full disclosure," I reply. "I never finished my dissertation. After graduate school and before teaching yoga, I ran my own executive search business and then, for twenty years, was a private school admissions director." I wonder what he thinks of my improbable career path. He doesn't say.

Finally, he proposes that we speak on the phone "because we might exhaust one another by writing such long essays."

He calls at 5 p.m. on Friday. *He sounds just like a college profes-sor*, I think. Voice deep and resonant, consonants articulated at the end of each word: "This is John-uh Pollock-uh." We set up a dinner date at a small restaurant in Jenkintown, where we will discover our mutual love of scallops, quinoa, and beet salad.

"I haven't been on a date since I was nineteen," I say on the phone.

"Then you are still nineteen years old," he replies.

My belly flips. I giggle, surprising myself.

*

I am hoping he finds me attractive in my blue cashmere sweater with the cowl neck, plaid skirt, and knee-high black leather boots. He shows up for that first date in a navy-blue blazer, oxford shirt, and khakis. We both have the same idea: tasteful, understated, not too showy.

Sitting across from him at the small table for two with our beet salads, waiting for him to say something, I notice his tortoiseshell-rimmed glasses are smudged, with a big scratch on the left lens, so it is hard to see his eyes as he regales me with stories of his mother growing up in China. Finally, I feel his eyes on me.

"I was attracted to that bright-eyed photo of you on the bike in your yellow sweater," he says, pushing his plate aside with half of his scallop entree uneaten. "I like happy, fit, athletic women."

I wonder if John and I will ever go biking together.

"I have an old Schwinn in the garage," he says. Later, I discover you can't open his garage door because twenty years of stuff falls out into the driveway.

Our dinner lasts four hours. There is something endearing about him, but I have no idea what he thinks of me, what he sees through those smudged, scratched glasses.

I don't hear from him.

Days later, I text him. "I really enjoyed our dinner together,"

I write. Then I go for broke: "I think you are handsome, a gentleman, and a great storyteller." I am piling it on.

"Now I am blushing," he texts back.

Okay, he likes me. He's a busy professor. Going forward, I decide to play the nineteen-year-old and allow him to set the pace. I feel off-kilter, unsure.

Two weeks later, I prepare to travel alone to my beloved yoga retreat in Tulum, Mexico, for the second year in a row, hoping to get back in balance with my yoga practice. *I will double down on my love letters to Herb*, I think.

I send a text to John. "I am going to Tulum. What color shall I paint my toenails?"

"Ask an Episcopalian, you'll get purple every time," he says.

Aroused in Tulum

I sit by the sea in an open-air dining pavilion, sipping coffee and watching the palm fronds rustle in the fresh morning breeze. I came here hoping to reinvigorate my yoga practice, yet I notice that the coconuts hanging from the trees look like testicles. I see genitalia everywhere. Yes, I am aroused by the possibility of a new boyfriend. I walk along the shoreline and vibrate with the pulsating surf. When I swim, my body undulates, buoyed up by the high salinity of the hot tropical sea. The water stirs me, enlivens me. I send a text to John, thinking I should be writing to Herb.

"I am aroused here," I say.

"And we haven't even held hands," he says.

I imagine sleeping with him under the mosquito netting in my Tulum cabana. I text him a photo of the bed. He hasn't even seen my apartment back home. I can fantasize, can't I?

"Fantasy precedes reality," Herb loved to say.

*

I walk along the beach to our thatched-roof "palapa" for Morning Meditation. Sun up, light soft, air still cool. Today, we partner up to lead one another like seeing eye dogs across Maya Tulum to the seashell-strewn labyrinth at the water's edge. I smile shyly at my partner, Sarah, young and lean with shiny black hair in a pale pink tank top, whom I am meeting for the first time today. I take her outstretched hand and close my eyes. I grip the still-cool sand with my toes, aware of the gentle rise and fall, twists and turns in the path. She speaks gently and firmly: "Turn here … a dip in the path … palm fronds overhead." They tickle my shoulders. I giggle, holding her hand tightly, like a child, sensing her hesitation, shifts in direction. As we enter the labyrinth, the sand grows warmer, less packed, deeper under foot. I hear the nearby crashing surf, smell it, the sun stronger now, hot on my face, shoulders, and arms. Eyes open now, I let go of Sarah's hand, whisper, "Thank you," and walk on my own along this spiraling nautilus in the sand.

*

The next morning, it is still dark, stars winking at me against the black velvet predawn Tulum sky. At first light, I will accompany my newly widowed friend Nell as she scatters the ashes of her husband, Manuel, from a promontory of rocks jutting into the sea.

I think of Herb in his Ziplock bag.

Nell says, tremulous and teary-eyed, "I believe the tides off the coast of Tulum will carry Manuel back to Cuba, where he was born." Though Nell and I have just met, I recognize in her sad eyes and downturned mouth the fragility and darkness I once knew so well. I feel the sting of her grief, the ache of her missing. I hear it in her trembling voice, remembering the day the children and I scattered Herb's ashes in our backyard with that stainless steel coffee scoop.

"We shall trust in wind and current to carry Manuel home to his final resting place," I say, my hand gentle on Nell's shoulder.

I recall Lydia's words: "It's just bones. Dad's bones carried him through life, and now he doesn't need them anymore."

What don't *I* need anymore? One year ago, my first in Tulum, I was still folded in on myself, trapped in that same gauzy cocoon of sadness that I see enveloping Nell. Since last year, I have sold our house and moved. I became a certified yoga instructor. I have John waiting back home. Here in Tulum, I dash into the waves and dance with friends to Mariachi music. I feel lighter. Writing daily love letters to Herb keeps me afloat like a life raft.

Blueberry Kefir

Home from Tulum and barely unpacked, I call John, who asks if he can visit me in my apartment on his way home from an alumni event at Swarthmore College. First time meeting not in a public place! I pour two wine glasses with wild blueberry kefir and await his arrival, sitting on the well-worn brown velvet flame stitch couch Herb and I bought in the seventies as newlyweds. I look around my apartment, a shrine to Herb. Pictures of him everywhere. Family photos from the kids' Bar and Bat Mitzvahs. Herb's lifetime achievement award from the Regional Council of Child and Adolescent Psychiatry. Herb as a Gerber baby with a curl on top of his head, a sweet little boy with his brother Steve, with me on our thirtieth anniversary atop glaciers in British Columbia, and our wedding. I worry how John will feel, surrounded by Herb and the life he and I shared.

Minutes after he arrives, we are on the couch, kissing like teenagers at a drive-in movie, wild blueberry kefir untouched on the coffee table. I am not ready for this at all. I sleep with him anyway. I feel like I am cheating on Herb. I keep my eyes closed the whole time. His body feels so different from Herb's—more girth. Until this moment, Herb's lean, long-limbed torso is the only body I've ever known. As we lay there in post-coital stupor, John starts to snore, which startles me because he sounds exactly like Herb. Then he wakes up and says, "I think of this as *simmering*."

Later, I serve us hearty vegetable soup that I have simmering on the stove. I notice something I had forgotten—how much I've missed cooking for my man, the way Herb always said "M-m-m-m" after the first bite. We linger for hours at the table, talking into the night. John asks if he could sleep over. This morning, I serve him raspberries and blueberries topped with a mixture of yogurt, almond butter, honey, and a sprinkle of walnuts.

"Gorgeous," he says at breakfast, "the way you combine flavors, textures, and colors."

Then we make love again. I still can't open my eyes.

"I love your gorgeous body," he says afterward. "Our bodies *like* each other!"

I can't imagine Herb would be okay with all this. I can't imagine John is okay with all those pictures of Herb around my apartment. I wonder if John will wake up one day and realize I'm not nineteen, not so gorgeous. Or worse, that he will die and leave me alone again.

My Dearest Love, Herb:

I never expected John to be so interested in you.

Back on that first phone call, he asked, "What did your husband do?"

On our first date, his opening question was, "How did your husband die?"

Yesterday morning, after our first sleepover together, I sat at the dining room table, still in my red plaid nightgown with little bows on the pockets, writing to you. John came out of the bedroom, wrinkled undershirt askew, and stood watching me with crinkled, sleepy eyes. Looking up at his tousled white curls, I saw concern on his face.

"I do this every morning," I said, wiping away my tears. "May I read you one of my letters to Herb?"

"Sure," he said, taking a seat across from me, folding his hands, waiting.

I sniffed, cleared my throat, hesitated, and said, "It must be strange dating a woman who writes daily love letters to her deceased husband."

"I do not see Herb as a rival," John said. "He is proof of the deep love you can feel for a man. I am grateful for Herb."

My shoulders relaxed, my belly softened, and I took a deep breath. Flipping through my journal, I found the letter about the morning I opened the box of your ashes and remembered yelling at your birthday flowers while writing your obituary. The tears flowed once more as I began to read. John sat in silence, eyes closed, attentive. I could *feel* his listening.

Later, he told me he loves all the photos of you and our family on every wall of my apartment. "I'm a family guy," he said, "and Herb looks so happy with you and the kids."

I marveled at the possibility that I could have found not one but two such big-hearted men in one lifetime.

Baby, was it you who sent John to me?

Tender-Hearted Men Who Snore

I've been here before, and it's not just his snoring, I think.

We're sitting at breakfast in my dining room, John on his third cup of coffee, and I realize there is something familiar in John's penchant for storytelling. I remember Herb telling the same joke over and over, cracking himself up so much he couldn't finish the joke. John, too, repeats the same story again and again and bursts out laughing before anyone can decide if it's funny. He loves to start a sentence with "as you know," when usually you don't, and end it with "as it were," signaling irony.

"John," I say, "you use the subjunctive so much I am going to write as your epitaph: *He was very fond of the subjunctive.*" He guffaws. I love that he can laugh at himself.

Epitaph? Uh-oh. I must be falling in love.

John is Scottish. His tender heart belies his massive physicality. He is barrel-chested with narrow hips and long, sinewy legs. There is girth around his middle, thickness in his neck, and a pleasant pudginess in his hands and feet. His shoulders and arms are muscle-bound from decades of playing tennis, as are his quads and glutes from so many years on the ski slopes of Colorado. He walks like he just got off a horse.

His eyes grow moist when he hears an aria, a boy choir, or a poem by Robert Burns. Then he heads out to the tennis courts to hurl top spins and insults at his buddies. "It's how men show they like each other," he says.

Last night, after dinner, candles sputtering on the table, John began to sing the "Skye Boat Song" softly, as he once sang his boys to sleep when they were little:

Speed, bonnie boat, like a bird on the wing.
Onward, the sailors cry!
Carry the lad who was born to be King
Over the sea to Skye.

Herb sang "Jeremiah Was a Bullfrog" to our kids at bedtime, thumping their mattresses like bongo drums: *Joy to the fishes in the deep blue sea / Joy to you and me.*

I wonder what it is that draws me to strong, tender-hearted men who sing to their children, who find beauty in sadness and longing.

Dare I fall in love again and risk losing John as I once lost Herb?

I can't bear writing another obituary.

Out of Place in Prague

Back in my morning perch on the balcony, I gaze at the pale green fuzz atop the just-opening trees in the distance. The dawn sky is pale white, but the horizon is painted hot pink against mottled gray as the sun, a diva, readies herself backstage amid much fanfare to make her daily appearance. "The world is full of promise, pregnant with life," Herb said every April, his favorite time of year.

Today's news: John is going to present a paper and facilitate a panel of scholars next month at an international communications studies conference in Prague and asked me to go with him! Should I?

Like the trees bursting into bud, I teeter on the edge, peering off into what might be—a new life with John, a trip to Prague.

Yes, go! I hear Herb say, as if he is whispering to me through the trees. It will take me another week to decide as the canopy unfolds. Something is holding me back. How well do I really know John to be taking such a long, expensive trip so far away from my home turf? I should be saving my money for Lydia's wedding, and what if she needs me around to help? It's true, too, that I am afraid to leave my mother. It was only three years ago that she fainted at The Talking Teacup in Chalfont, and we raced over to drive her to Abington Hospital, where she checked out against medical advice after insulting the chief of cardiology. Now, she says, the beta blockers make her woozy.

"Hi, Mom."

"Hi, babe."

"How are you?"

"Okay." *Can I believe her?*

"I am going to Prague with John. Just for five days," I say, surprising myself.

"Have fun!"

She seems okay. *I will go!*

Packing, I picture John in Princeton rummaging through the piles of laundry on his bedroom floor, looking for two socks that match, searching through overstuffed closets for the right piece of luggage. Herb and I would have shared a suitcase. I will accessorize my one dressy plum suit with a couple of scarves and necklaces. I wonder, what does a "professor's wife" wear? Like my roller bag, I feel light and small, about to enter someplace big and strange. On departure day, John arrives packed and ready to go, wearing his cowboy hat and thrilled that our SEPTA train to the airport is free for seniors. In the terminal, we stop at a sushi bar, and I imagine we are on our first date. Again.

*

The overnight plane to Dublin has not yet reached cruising altitude, and John is already nodding off, chin dropping into a Velcro-wrapped Trtl neck pillow he bought for this trip—one for him, one for me. My ears are popping on the ascent, and I know they will pop more on the descent as I listen for the reassuring grind of the landing gear some seven hours from now. I wrap the Trtl around my neck, take it off, and put it on, and I can't get comfortable. I swivel my butt in the airplane seat, hitting the armrests on either side, knees touching the tray table in front. John, six inches taller than me, is completely wedged in, hips and knees splayed open. He spritzed his tray table and hands with sanitizer as soon as we boarded, passing it to me. *No thanks. I prefer soap and water.* We joked about "doing it" in the airplane bathroom. I can feel the heat of his body next to mine. An involuntary quiver rises in me at the thought of us in a hotel room for five consecutive nights in an exotic foreign country. He says I am the first girlfriend, partner, or wife, even (he's been married twice), to accompany him to a professional conference. Maybe he surprised himself when he invited me.

I surprised myself when I said, "Yes, I'll go." John is my first traveling companion since Herb died two years ago, and it feels so good not to be flying alone. On our second date just weeks ago, John regaled me with tales of travel to India, where he interned with the U.S. Foreign Service while in graduate school. As a professor, he said, he brought groups of students to South Africa two years in a row. This worldly new man in my life has seen so much, knows so much. It was like that with Herb, too.

My first time flying over the Atlantic, I was twenty-two, like John when he went to India. Alone on a plane to Avignon via Paris to attend graduate classes on Baudelaire and *Surréalisme*, I was scared and heartsick, having left behind my then medical school boyfriend to his summer job as a prep orderly, shaving pubic hair. In Avignon, I wrote detailed letters to Herb every morning and evening as if practicing, honing the habit of mystical connection with an absent loved one. In 1973, the flimsy airmail stationery crinkled like onion skin, designed to keep down the cost of trans-Atlantic postage, like the matching paper-thin envelopes bordered with red and blue stripes. To save money, my handwriting was microscopic. At summer's end, Herb flew over to join me, proposing marriage along the *Promenade des Anglais* in Nice. We were never apart after that, so the letter-writing stopped. Until he died, and I picked up where I left off.

But oh, to be going back to Europe again. Twenty-three hours in transit, and I will not sleep a wink—never could, sitting up in an airplane. I stare at the words above my tray table,

"Use seat cushion as flotation device." Too tired to read and too wired to sleep, I default to my favorite pastime, reflection. Through the haze of weary wakefulness and dimmed cabin lights, I delight in having someone to trust again, here at our cruising altitude of thirty-five thousand feet. I have no idea where I am going with him, this Energizer-bunny man who claims he must have ten hours' sleep a night plus his afternoon nap. *Must be because, the rest of the time, his busy brain is in overdrive.* It calms me as it always does to see John so deeply asleep and arouses in me a longing to be able to sleep like that, even on a plane. I can hear his rhythmic snoring over the din of the airplane's engine. I smile, lean into his shoulder. Damn armrest. Damn flickering blue light from someone's laptop across the aisle.

It is now 3 a.m. in Philly (I refuse to reset my watch). I am out of place, out of time, somewhere over the Atlantic in this pressurized metal tube, and I am sure I smell gravy and mashed potatoes. Trays of dinner appear out of nowhere, which feels so wrong. John wakes up and mechanically shovels portions of beef stew into his mouth before falling back asleep, and I nibble on the stew, although we already ate sushi in the Philly airport. Two hours later, I smell coffee as sunlight pours in around the edges of the window shades, and more trays arrive with breakfast. *Please, no more food.* John blinks awake and stows his Trtl while I peek through the glass to behold the shimmering coast of Ireland below, like the green of a child's acrylic paint set. It's just too soon for sunrise.

Or am I entirely too late? For all of this. To be a professor's trailing spouse?

John fears we will be too late for our connecting flight to Prague, so I trail behind him as we sprint through Dublin airport. It feels great to be stretching my legs, and I am loving the lilt of the Irish brogue on the PA system as we dash along, with me wishing we could stay here where I understand the language. Three weeks ago, John bought me two guidebooks about Prague, *The Lonely Planet* and *Rick Steves*, "because each one emphasizes different things to see," John said. There are survival phrases in both books which I tried to memorize but have no idea how to pronounce. Landing in Prague, I see signage that could mean "customs" or "immigration" or "baggage claim" or "ground transportation" or something else entirely. It is morning in Philadelphia, afternoon in the Czech Republic. Suddenly, ears still ringing, I am deplorably incurious about the city of Prague. I want more than anything to sleep horizontally on a real pillow, not in a Trtl.

*

Jet lag is my liminal space, in which Herb is a memory and John is still mostly an idea. Today, and for the next five days in Prague, John will materialize into an actual guy with clothes and toiletries and peacock pride and irritable moments and daily habits.

Still holding our luggage after twenty-three hours in transit, travel-weary John and I stand together at the foot of the small double bed at the boutique Hotel Opera in Prague, a pink-and-white five-story edifice that takes up an entire city block. Awash in gargoyles, Corinthian colonnades, and Romanesque arches, it has a cupola on the roof, a distinctive landmark visible from all directions, which I will come to appreciate each time I venture out and panic that I've gotten lost.

Inside, the rooms are tiny, with barely room for a small table and one chair. Not even a closet. I don't care. John, I am about to find out, never unpacks, just leaves his suitcase open on the floor and rummages through it. But the windows are large, and the May sunlight streams in. "It's charming," I say, a bit unconvincingly. John picked it out because it is cheaper than the big hotels. We seem to be the only Americans here.

"Which side of the bed do you want?" he asks tentatively. With Herb, I always slept on the right. I point woodenly to the left because that's the side I'm on, and he puts his glasses, phone, keys, day timer, and portable CPAP machine on the right bedside table.

I go to pee in the tiny bathroom and see John's vast array of toiletries already spread around the sink—lotions and potions and gadgets and pills, with no room for my toothbrush.

This is how it's going to be, I think, and step into my new life on the left side of the bed with a man who has lots of stuff and snores just like Herb.

I love hearing him snore.

Not sure about all that stuff spilling out of his suitcase. I hope he still wants his yoga-teacher girlfriend around while he hobnobs with scholars from all over the world. I am winging it here, off-kilter, trying to get my bearings, not just in Prague but wherever I am, since Herb died.

*

What am I doing halfway around the world knowing my eighty-nine-year-old mother could need me at any moment back in Philly? *She said she was okay.* What am I doing with a man I barely know (but yearn to know) in a city where I don't speak the language, can't even pronounce the street signs? John took off early this morning, as he will for the next two days, to work at the conference. Dapper in his gray suit, monogrammed shirt, blue silk necktie, and cowboy hat, he asked me to fold his matching handkerchief so it sticks out of his breast pocket just so.

In my yoga pants and sneakers, I am on my own to explore this ancient fairytale city, studying the guidebooks John gave me—like a college assignment—to scope out places for us to visit together over the weekend. "Find us some concert tickets!" he calls over his shoulder on his way out the door. Is he barking at me?

Clinging to my map and a guidebook, I set out towards the river. I memorize landmarks—a warehouse, a pub, a billboard—as I get further from the pink hotel so I can find my way back without panicking. I follow the Vltava River in search of the iconic Charles Bridge. Trees bloom in soft colors along the banks of the river. The air smells fresh, damp, and dewy. The spring morning is cool, and I quicken my pace, the bridge coming into view—ancient statues silhouetted against the dappled sky. Spires, turrets, and crenelations everywhere. I climb up the embankment into the old city, lured down narrow passageways, afraid to take my eye off the river lest I get turned around and lose my way home. For a split second, I think I am lost.

"Mom doesn't know left from right," my children told John. Herb would have agreed.

And she's terrified of getting lost. Always has been. But now, maybe the bigger danger is falling in love again. Wishes and fears all tangled up together in this unfamiliar city.

Rounding a corner, I spy a poster on a crumbling stone wall announcing a concert Saturday night at the Mirror Chapel, where Mozart played the organ. I snag two tickets inside the church and jog home along the river, hoping I don't miss the turn-off to the hotel. Ah, there's my warehouse, pub, and billboard. They look different coming from this direction. My pink hotel looks strange from the back, too—no gargoyles. I hesitate, about to panic, then round the corner: the cupula, gargoyles! Hotel Opera!

*

According to my guidebook, Prague is the city of Kafka, Dvorak, and Mozart. Herb would have loved seeing so many ancient synagogues cheek-in-jowl with medieval churches, as this is one of the few European cities not bombed to rubble in World War II. Prague is unfolding before me as a cultural layer cake with filigree icing, castles, and soaring cathedrals, a crossroads linking East and West, past and present, monarchies and Communists. To Herb, it would have been a memorial to the Holocaust. My Jewish friends back home would ask, *What? You didn't visit Theresienstadt, where 263,000 Czech Jews died? No*, I think, *I cannot ask John to visit a concentration camp. Or perhaps it is I who cannot bear to see the horror.*

But on Sunday, when I ask John if we can visit the Prague synagogues and he says yes, I will feel closer to him than ever before as I straddle my two worlds, Jewish and non-Jewish. I do not yet know how on Sunday afternoon I will stand beside John transfixed, unable to breathe, inside the Pinkas Synagogue where the names of all 263,000 murdered Czech Jews are inscribed along the walls and the artwork of children incarcerated in Theresienstadt is displayed under glass. I will want to read each name. *You lived; you mattered. You artists and poets and musicians. You children. You would-have-been Dvoraks, Kafkas, and Mozarts. Beautiful souls snuffed out.* I will avert my eyes, unable to speak or move, and, with the wordless reverence I will come to love about him, John will feel it too, will understand.

Saturday night. We climb to the tiny balcony, mirrors refracting the light around us, and John says, "Can you imagine a young Mozart playing that organ in 1789?" A young soprano in a purple gown with spaghetti straps glides forward into the spotlight and begins Dvorak's "Song to the Moon." I hear a sudden change in John's breathing, a catch in his throat as she crescendos. I look over. His eyes are welling up, glistening. His right hand lands softly in my lap. I lean into his body. He takes my hand.

Suddenly, I know in my heart I am meant to be in Prague right now: a new city, a new man, a new song. From this moment forward, John anoints "Song to the Moon" as our forever theme song. He will never tire of hearing it.

He will never tire, as well, of talking about our random

subway and street corner encounters and how we became an "us" in Prague, our "first time out in public." We are heading off to see the sights on a crowded subway when a man seated across the car from us is smiling broadly at John. "Finland's top communication scholar," John says above the roar. Exiting the train, he approaches John by the escalator and says, "I've been following your groundbreaking research on community structure theory since the nineteen seventies." John blushes. Over time, I will learn that this "community structure theory" has been and will always be John's life work and legacy.

Next, on a busy street corner five blocks from the Hotel Opera near the subway stop, another man smiles at John. "Nobody does more than you," he says, "to encourage under-graduates to enter our field." John demurs. "No," the colleague insists, "you are a legend!" More blushing.

"We were Ph.D. candidates together back at Stanford," John explains to me and turns to his colleague, extending an arm in my direction with a flourish: "*This* is my girlfriend, Peggy." I wanted to curtsey like a debutante; I was being *presented*.

Later, John will joke, "I'm sure you thought I arranged these random encounters just to impress you." I will pretend that he had, again, with each retelling.

*

As we board our flights back to the US, this time through Heathrow, Prague follows us home like our very own foundation story. The hustle and bustle of Heathrow reminds me of Times Square, and I no longer care that English is spoken here. Crowds jostle us as we sprint past a warren of gates to make our connection to Philadelphia. We will go backward in time, following the sun on its westward arc. It will be 4 a.m. in Prague when we arrive home. Home to my big bed where John will again take up residence on Herb's side. I know I will not sleep until then. John will nap peacefully every hour or so, wrapped in his Trtl once again.

Ladies and gentlemen, the captain has turned on the fasten seat-belt sign in preparation for take-off. A flight attendant peers into my lap. *Click.* The cold metal of the buckle presses uncomfortably on my belly button. I unclick and try again, threading the strap so the belt is longer, looser. Too loose now: I am not protected against "unexpected turbulence." I could get a concussion hitting my tray table stowed in its upright position. I pull the strap tighter and try to wiggle in my seat. Just right.

I look over at John, already absorbed in his novel. Sensing my gaze, he pats my hand, smiles, and turns the page. I feel like I've known him forever. Like the familiar press of the seatbelt against my abdomen, he is a presence, a benign protector, close by. I slide my hand under the metal clasp, lift it away from my body, then let it drop to rest on my belly, and there it will stay for the duration. I may forget about it, but know it is there.

I giggle.

"What?" John says.

"The Sorcerer's Apprentice."

He guffaws.

In our tiny Hotel Opera bathroom, in lieu of a shower head, was a hand-held hose that flipped wildly as soon as you turned on the water, soaking the entire room. You couldn't control it and wash yourself at the same time. I tried holding it between my knees while soaping up, but it escaped, shooting water all over the ceiling and walls and onto the toilet. "Just like 'The Sorcerer's Apprentice' in *Fantasia*," John said.

Because we are flying westward, that giant yellow orb doesn't seem to be moving across the sky as on a normal day. It just hangs, staying with us. Or *we* are staying with *it*. Near the end of the flight, the sun finally dips towards the horizon. John dozes. My eyes close. My head drops on his shoulder. I rest my hands on the metal clasp below my waist. It feels warm now. It holds me. I don't want the plane to land.

Our first night back in my apartment, John asks, "Can we listen to 'Song to the Moon?'" We search YouTube and find a live performance by his favorite singer, Renee Fleming. He watches the screen, and I watch his face. His eyes change color like limpid pools. I want to swim in them.

The next day, we resume our separate lives. John leaves for three weeks in Aspen, a summer trip planned before we met.

Still a Daughter

"Mom," Lydia says on the phone on my first day home, urgency in her voice, "visit Nana. Something has changed in her." I delay for a day or two. There's laundry to do.

On Sunday, I visit my mother at home. We settle across from one another at the blue-and-white Delft-tiled kitchen table—vitamins, coffee cup, Tastykake lemon pie, and utensils already set out for tomorrow's breakfast. Everything looks normal. Her "to-do" list by the telephone says *nails, ironing, Peggy at 1:00.*

"How is John? How was Prague?" she asks. I am moved, surprised that she cares, but it's not like my teenage days when I'd ramble on and on and she'd listen. These days, she just wants to talk about herself. I can't tell exactly what she can hear. Growing old must be so scary.

Then I watch Mom struggle to stand, to walk. I notice that her once confident stride has become more of a shuffle during the week I was away. This alarms me. I sense that my time with her is running out. We move to the den, half-completed crossword puzzles arranged across her rattan coffee table. No crossword puzzle dictionary for her. "That's cheating!" she says. She moves in slow motion. "More time to think," she says. I sit beside her on the same sofa that once stood opposite the fireplace in my childhood living room, where I put coal in my brothers' Christmas stockings.

"What are you most proud of?" I ask her.

"Nothing," she says, a shadow crossing her face.

"Try a different answer," I say gently. I wait.

She sits in silence, breathing with a wheeze after years of smoking.

"I think," she begins haltingly, "I think what I am most proud of is having had the courage to leave your father."

My belly flips at the mention of *the divorce* even now. A perennially simmering conflagration that compelled us five children to declare our loyalty, feeling shame for secretly loving the other parent who was also part of who we were, a shame that cut off part of ourselves from ourselves.

That's it? I think. *The only thing you are proud of?*

First, I watch the trembling in her lower lip. I look again and notice the set of her jaw, her primly folded hands: I see courage, sureness, resolve. It was always there, but I never saw it.

Slowly, I nod and feel my own face soften as it dawns on me how truly hard it was for her, alone with five children, to leave her husband of twenty-five years, never to marry again. Something uncoils in my stomach. It hits me like a gut-punch: how much and how long she suffered in that marriage. She *needed* to end it.

Several minutes pass. We sit in relaxed silence. She stands, smiling, and says, "This has been a good day!" I want more than anything to be the reason for her good day. *Are good days few and far between for you, Mom?* We stand facing one another. Once, she was two inches taller than me. Am I taller now? I see softness in her face, her auburn hair, her green-hazel eyes, her pale blue cotton shirt, perfectly ironed. *I still have a mother.*

We hug good-bye. Her back feels fragile under my yoga-strong hands.

After I drive off, she prepares to take her nightly bath.

On Monday, her neighbor calls to say Mom hasn't picked up her newspaper.

She always picks up her newspaper.

I ask the neighbor to call 911, and the medics find Mom

naked, lying in the empty tub, confused, dehydrated, and her skin desiccated. I race to meet the ambulance in the ER at Chestnut Hill Hospital, where Mom cannot remember what happened.

"I was naked in front of those strange men. They were all over my house," she says to me when I find her on a gurney in the ER.

"Who is the President of the United States?" a doctor asks her.

"He's not my president," she says.

*

Mom shouts, "Take these off!" Green eyes flashing, auburn hair askew.

"You know I can't," I say, inches from her hospital bed where I had been standing daily for four days. Today would have been my forty-fourth wedding anniversary. I am remembering that years ago, Herb diagnosed my mother as "oppositional." He should see her now! John calls nightly from Aspen, solicitous and concerned but worlds away.

"I'm not talking to you," Mom says, turning her head away from me, flattening her perfect pageboy.

"Choose your battles," I sigh, sad that turning her head is all she has left.

Bulky white mitts are taped over her hands to prevent her from pulling out her IV, which she did twice during the night and again this morning. Now, she is ripping the mitts off with her teeth. Yesterday, I stepped out of her room to take a call, and when I came back, blood was everywhere, all over the sheets. She had ripped out her IV. Nurses changed her bedding and wrapped her in mitts all the way up to her elbows, concealing her perfectly manicured peach-colored fingernails, which she always polished herself. Toenails matching. She never had a mani-pedi in her life. Colored her own hair. Auburn with a tinge of purple. Pageboy. Not a hair out of place. Until now.

It takes two people to move Mom anywhere: bed to chair, bed to commode.

"What a difference a day makes," she says, having driven to the Dollar Tree last Sunday to stock up on air freshener shortly before I arrived for our final visit. Soon, I would discover thirty unopened air fresheners in her front hall closet. Now, at Chestnut Hill Hospital, where all four of her sons were born, I can see she is slipping away, cheeks sunken, face pinched, hair disheveled, mitts on her hands like boxing gloves. I run my finger along her waist where the plastic diaper irritates her skin. I can feel the ridges of stretch marks across her abdomen from her five babies. She gained eighty pounds with the twins. As I stroke her belly with my fingertips, her jaw unclenches. I continue to move my fingers back and forth lightly, like raindrops. Her agitated breathing slows, quiets.

Today, I am taking our housekeeper, Yonka, to clean up the urine-soaked chaos in Mom's bathroom before my brothers get here. I ask my brother Andy to drive up from Maryland and stay with Mom while I'm out cleaning. He comes immediately. I love him for that.

In her hospital bed, Mom yells incoherently.

"That's *exactly* what you did to me when I was a little boy," Andy says, mostly to himself.

"You deserved it!" she says, suddenly lucid, green eyes on fire, then dimming as she drops off to sleep, snoring raggedly.

One by one, the family arrives—Lexi, Tommy, Jake, Zach, Lydia, and Dan—the six eldest grandchildren—and my brother Pete, who never missed a Sunday morning call with her. "Peach Cake," she called him, and only him. I intercept Pete at the hospital elevator, fresh off his red eye from Seattle, to prepare him for Mom's deteriorating, delirious state. The color drains from his lips. He walks into her room expecting the worst. "Hi, Peach Cake!" Mom says brightly. I roll my eyes and shrug at Pete. He shrugs back.

*

"I don't want Mom alone in the hospital without family there," I say, planning her transfer to hospice after the doctors at Chestnut Hill Hospital say there is nothing more they can do. Andy's son Tommy is the first to volunteer to stay all night with her.

Tommy calls me at 3 a.m., his voice shaking, "*She's going. She nibbled on the Tastykake lemon pie we brought her. I was playing her favorite Broadway tunes from* Avenue Q *on my cell phone, and she was swaying to the music. Now, the nurse says she's going.*"

I run into my guest room to awaken Dan, hard to rouse in his eye mask and ear plugs. We dash to the car and speed over to the hospital, a twenty-minute drive, arriving in ten minutes, only possible at 3 a.m.

We sprint through the revolving hospital doors as my phone rings again.

"She's *gone*," Tommy sobs.

Mom's night nurse meets us at her room.

"Your mom was very lucky," she says. I gaze at Mom, motionless in her bed, lips parted, looking like she's about to say something, auburn pageboy framing her frozen face. "I've worked on this unit for many years. Ninety-five percent of these old, very sick patients die alone with no one there. Your mother had her grandson Tommy right by her side. Beautiful to see."

Family shows up, Herb taught me by example.

I hold Tommy in my arms, hug and hug and hug him, wishing I could squeeze the sadness out of him. I peek over at Mom's chart. *Cause of death*, it says, *failure to thrive.*

It is Tuesday. Herb died on a Tuesday, too.

9 a.m. I drive home slowly, windows down, air honeysuckle sweet, June sun shining, no need to rush. *You did it, Mom! I think. You died on your terms. With dignity. No muss, no fuss—well,*

just a little. It's been decades since I needed you, confided in you. I used to,
though. You were the best listener.

I pull into the parking lot at The Plaza, having sped away
to the hospital in the dark at 3 a.m. Suddenly, I am too tired
to get out of the car.

John calls from Aspen. "Do you want me to come back
for the funeral?" I wish with all my heart that he would. And
already feel the awkwardness if he did.

"Nah. Thanks, but you just got there, and besides, you
barely knew her." John met her twice, last time over lunch
at my place for Mother's Day. "She sure says *no* a lot," John
said as we washed the dishes. "I would have a hard time with
such an oppositional mother." I felt like a long-suffering saint
when he said that, but I wanted them to like each other. Just
before Mother's Day, the three of us attended an art preview
together. I was embarrassed when Mom yelled "No!" at him
for trying to take her arm in the parking lot. When, after
twenty minutes, John ducked into the men's room, my mother
whispered, "You and John are alike."

"What do you mean?"

"You are both great listeners." I couldn't wait to tell John.

Now, Mom has said *no* for the last time, met the man in
my life for the last time. John is in Aspen, and I am simply
empty. Next week, and for the next several weeks, I will clean
out her fridge, her stove, her garage, her basement, her closets, her cabinets, her entire house. Tenderly, as if I were still
stroking her belly.

It will be ten months before I shed my first tear. I will
be back in Tulum, galloping into the womb of the ocean and
swimming due east into the just-risen sun, tasting the warm
salty water, that river of life, the amniotic soup that gave birth
to all creatures great and small. Me. I will think of her, and
suddenly, from deep inside, a wail of grief will emit in a voice
I do not recognize, followed by gasping, shuddering.

I will howl like a wolf baying at the moon. The way Mom

locked herself in the laundry room and howled for three days after Dad moved out. She thought the banging and clanging of the washer and dryer would drown her out, but I heard her high-pitched keening. Now, I will be swimming and sobbing, hot tears blending with the warm salty water. "Mo-o-o-o-o-o-o-m," I will wail, "I miss you. Thank you, thank you, thank you for my life. For everything that you were, that you gave: the love, the love." In the end, I will swim the backstroke, stare at the impossibly blue sky, and sing, "I don't know why you say, 'Good-bye', I say, 'Hello, hello, hello' / I don't know why you say, 'Good-bye', I say, 'Hello'."

The House of Tomorrow

I will think often, now that he is no longer here, *How would Herb have handled this?* The silver lining of dying while the world continues to spin on its axis, as it does, is that we miss whatever brings pain and suffering after we are gone. Herb missed the death of his mother-in-law, whose grief over his untimely death she bore like the loss of a child. "I just know your mother is going to outlive me," he said often. Right again.

Two weeks before he died, Herb took Dan and Lydia one at a time into the living room to ask them where they thought they would be in five years. The formal living room in our house, as for so many in our generation, was the one room we didn't "live" in. Except for piano lessons (weekly) and kids practicing piano (hardly ever). We saved this room, with its fancy, perishable Chinese tufted area rug—no food allowed—for company. The other exception was when Herb took one of our children in there for the dreaded "talk" after they committed an egregious transgression such as failing to weed the pachysandra when asked or lying about delivering the Jenkintown Times Chronicle to a neighbor on his paper route. The brown velvet flame-stitch couch became the "hot seat" where our children were captive, unable to escape their dad's accusatory gaze as he sat directly across from them in his overstuffed turquoise blue chair, also perishable and not for everyday rough housing with muddy feet.

On this day then, when Herb, so very sick, asked each of our now adult children to join him in the living room on that very same couch, they knew it was for something serious. It was always one-on-one; I was never privy. But I, too, felt the weightiness of this fraught location in our house each time Herb disappeared into that room with Dan or Lydia reluctantly in tow.

"Five years from now," Herb had said, "I want to imagine it," the kids would tell me years later when I asked about that day. They said they would never forget that conversation, a crucible of sorts. In hindsight, I believe Herb also wanted *them* to imagine it and, in his wise and gentle way, was helping them face life without a father, helping them to seal their own futures. *I'm not afraid of dying*, he told me, *but I can't stand leaving you and the kids.* I realize now Herb was both saying good-bye and assuring his children he would always be watching from his perch on the overstuffed turquoise blue chair.

Lydia told Herb she knew she would be marrying Jake and buying a home. Dan was already raising seed money to start his own business in genomics and told Herb he expected to find a special someone with whom to share it all. Within a year, Dan would call his biotech start-up "GRO Biosciences." Both children emerged from this living room chat red-eyed and sobbing but also, I sensed, calmer, having drawn strength from this man they knew loved them more than life itself.

"Our children dwell in the house of tomorrow, which we cannot visit, not even in our dreams," wrote Kalil Gibran. But Herb was determined to accompany his children into their futures as he looked death squarely in the eye, and they both would believe he was still there long after he was gone, feeling his presence. On cold nights in Boston, Dan would wrap himself in his dad's red and black checkered flannel shirt, rescued from Herb's closet after he died, and talk with his father about his first GRO Bio breakthrough—a new, genetically recoded, re-engineered enzyme that's never existed before, giving hope to immunocompromised patients. Lydia would want Herb to know how she became a much sought-after Licensed Massage Therapist in Philadelphia's most rigorous program and later a wildly successful, award-winning software marketer. Imagined conversations, both our kids as ardently believing Herb was listening as I did when I wrote my love letters. "I just know," Herb told me after the living room talk, "our children are going to grow from the experience of losing me. You, too," he said. *How did he know?*

The future kept happening. It keeps happening. Just after the one-year anniversary of Herb's death, Lydia and Jake are vacationing in Orlando, Florida. I am already in bed asleep, and the phone rings. It's Lydia erupting into peals of laughter, those tinkling bells, that contagious joy Herb and I couldn't get enough of: "Jake just proposed to me," she says, breathless. "On his knees. In a gazebo. Oh, Mama, wait till you see the ring. It's so pretty. I'll send pictures. Gotta go. Bye." Of course, I cannot sleep now. I am weeping, my face buried in Herb's pillow. *Oh, Herb, our girl. If only you were here for this.*

Are you?

They set their wedding date for eighteen months after that.

Still a Mother

Months before her wedding, I tell Lydia, "I know what you need from me. I can think of only two tasks as mother of the bride. One, help to minimize your stress. Two, don't do or say anything that would add to your stress." She nods with a wry little smile.

John is not around for these wedding preparations, but when I report back to him on my latest adventures with Lydia, this uncharted mother-of-the-bride territory feels a little less daunting. John finds my stories amusing but has said more than once it's a good thing he only has sons, because he is not sure he could have survived the drama of a girl's teenage years. I think he would have been a wonderful father to a girl.

Now, it is 6 a.m. on a hot summer morning.

I have gotten used to either driving alone or being the chauffeur again, but navigating interstate highways is nerve-wracking for me. Today's mission: a quest for the perfect wedding cake. I take off from my home in Jenkintown to South Philadelphia to pick up Lydia and her fiancé, Jake, so that we can then head north on the New Jersey Turnpike to New York City for a 9 a.m. rendezvous on 34th Street at the Madison Square Garden entrance to Penn Station. There, we will meet the baker of Lydia's gluten-free carrot cake for the wedding; she has prepared sample cupcakes for us to taste.

Jake is in the back seat in his signature camouflage baseball cap, navigating me with his cell phone. In the mirror, I can see the rectangular tattoo on his right bicep peeking out below his mustard shirtsleeve and an "F-hole" tattoo curlicued along his left triceps, cyclist's muscles bulging. Even-tempered and a man of few words, he is the perfect partner for my bubbly, chatterbox girl who wears her heart on her sleeve. Lydia, now a massage therapist, is strong and lean in her maroon tank top and khaki shorts. When she turns to reach for the knobs on my radio, I glimpse her tattoo of a pig in a heart behind her right shoulder strap. She hums continuously, perched where I used to sit when Herb drove us on family trips—he would have known exactly how to get to New York City. Jake, whom my brother Larry once called "mini-Herb" because of his calm demeanor, keeps me oriented.

We pull over in front of Penn Station at 8:55. Lydia calls the number for the baker, and a young brunette in high heels and a miniskirt emerges from the Penn Station escalator holding a white box tied with string. She hesitates next to our car. "Um, Lydia?" She passes the box through the passenger side window into Lydia's eagerly outstretched hands. Taxis are honking at us. I pray Lydia will like the cake as she unties the string and opens the box. A cinnamon smell fills the car. She bites into an orange cupcake with chunks of apple and buttercream frosting, passing it around to Jake and me. It is perfect.

We stop in Greenwich Village to meet Jeanette, one of Lydia's bridesmaids, who also tastes a cupcake. Eyes rolling back, she flashes a grin. Next, we take a hot walk on the High Line along the Hudson River in Chelsea, passing old meatpacking warehouses and factories repurposed into condominiums, pubs, and gyms. I marvel at the baby trees and shrubs the city has planted along this unusual urban park, once an elevated train line. John, who once worked for five years in New York City, would really enjoy this place—I will tell him all about it. And he will crack up, incredulous, when I recount the cupcake pilgrimage.

Finally, Jake navigates me back through the Holland Tunnel to the turnpike and home to South Philadelphia, where I drop off the bride and her groom with their remaining cupcakes. I drive another hour back north to my home. Seven hours in the car for a carrot cake.

*

Another day, Lydia and I arrive together at Anthropologie on Philadelphia's Rittenhouse Square. The ground floor in this ornate building is all bridal gowns and accessories, furnished like a nineteenth-century boudoir with Victorian couches, triple floor-to-ceiling mirrors, and flutes of champagne on silver trays on a coffee table for the brides-to-be and their entourages. A personal "wedding consultant" bustles back and forth with dresses for Lydia to try on—strapless, backless, sleeves off the shoulder, plunging necklines, silky, lacey, skin-tight, flowy, ivory, cream, off-white.

I am snapping pictures from various angles—front, back, side, hemline, décolletage. I send each picture to her phone and to her girlfriends' phones; they are standing by for comment. She'll know the dress she wants when she sees it. Later, she'll know what dress I should wear as mother-of-the-bride, and I will love it too—the tan one with the halter top and silver sequins. She'll snap a photo of me and send it to John. "Elegant," he'll say. At the dressmaker, we will be fitted for sewn-in bras. Lydia will call our breasts "the girls." I will ask the dressmaker if my bra could be placed any higher to give "the girls" a lift. "No," she will say, "that's where they are."

I love being mother of the bride to Lydia. We've giggled our way all over Philadelphia, looking for the perfect venue. We've had a tasty carrot cake adventure in New York City. We've been playing dress-ups at Anthropologie. We are amazed by the multitude of relatives from all over the country who immediately said "yes" to her hand-drawn invitation: a whimsical sketch of the two of them—Jake in his baseball cap—on their knees, shovel in hand, planting a heart-shaped bare root sapling. No one wants to miss this joyful celebration taking root after the wrenching loss of Herb; everyone Lydia and Jake invited is coming—not a single regret! The tent will be packed to capacity. There will be no leftover carrot cake.

Plus One

Lydia fills mason jars with fairy lights, an infinitesimal tangle of tiny orbs that grew brighter as the sun went down on her wedding night. She orders one hundred fifty live succulents, delivered to my apartment the Wednesday before the wedding. My job? To transplant each one, with two tablespoons of potting soil, into miniature metal pails with wire handles, half of them pink, half white. In my now-greenhouse living room, I use my smallest cream pitcher to deliver just the right amount of water into each pail—*keep the soil moist until Saturday.* My den is already floor-to-ceiling piles of boxes of wedding gifts and shower gifts, and my guest room closet is stacked with mason jars and batteries for the fairy lights. There are garlands of green ivy in bubble wrap and white picture frames for table settings named after herbs, all waiting to be assembled and delivered to the venue the Friday before the wedding. I fuss over the succulents, poking my pinky into the soil of each one in its tiny pail, careful not to disturb the fragile roots. *To water or not to water?*

On the day itself, I arise early, thinking of John, miles away in his study in Princeton, hunched over his desk in a dead heat to meet his publication deadlines so he can make it to the wedding tonight. After only six months together, John will be meeting Herb's relatives for the first time. I wonder how he feels about that. I wonder how I feel about that. But there is no time for reflection or flirtatious texting today, for him or me—our days are going to be equally long and very different.

I race downtown in the morning rush hour to the hotel, where the bridesmaids gather for "hair and make-up," stopping to pick up box lunches for them. John is no stranger to "hair and make-up," having appeared on *The Today Show* four times, but cannot fathom, when I tell him, why "hair and make-up" for a 5 p.m. wedding begins at 10 a.m. He never had a daughter.

We reconvene at Ridgeland Mansion in west Fairmount Park, still hours before I will see John again, the family coming together for the first time since Herb's funeral. It is a glorious September afternoon, the sky clearing after two weeks of rain. Bridesmaids fuss over Lydia in the bridal suite, feeding her bottled water and holding up her wedding dress as she gingerly steps in. The photographer bustles in and out. I sit quietly under a window and watch. There is nothing left for me to do. She knows I am there. Witness.

*

When guests start arriving, I am startled to spot John in the parking lot, alone, looking uncertain in his impeccable gray tailored suit and silver tie from Beijing. He is scanning the crowd, and I realize with a pang that he knows no one. With another pang, I excuse myself from the gaggle of Herb's many relatives and walk toward him, flashing a smile and a wave. I am feeling way more at home than he, reunited with family I've known forever, especially Herb's. I am worried about John and Herb's family, too. As John bends toward me and plants a kiss on my painted lips, I momentarily stiffen, thinking Herb's relatives are watching. "You look so elegant," John says, smiling. I forget the relatives and lean into his sturdy body. Grateful to have this kind man in my life, my own plus one, in a custom suit from Singapore.

"I'm putting you down for a plus one, Mom," Lydia had said, drafting her wedding guest list more than a year before

I met John. I shrugged, shook my head, and forgot about it. Now, John and I have been together for six months.

In the Ridgeland parking lot, he affably greets the blur of relatives–mine, Herb's, and Jake's. Though he immediately forgets their names, he will tear up during the ceremony as if he had always been part of our family.

"I love big, close-knit families," he tells me again.

*

A ceremony among ancient trees. My radiant, doe-eyed Lydia with her cherry lips and close-cropped brown curls waits at the edge of the glen in her cream-colored, off-the-shoulder, clingy lace dress while the wedding party processes. Arm in arm, Jake's mother and I walk in step with the music. We steady one another, then separate, taking our seats on opposite sides of the front row. I slide along the painted white wooden bench to where John sits waiting on my left, his suit jacket grazing my bare arm. I love him for being there, but I am distracted, praying that he understands how my two worlds, past and present, are colliding in this moment. I am back in that liminal space where Herb is present in his absence, John is still an idea unfolding, and my baby girl is slipping away. Later, John will acknowledge that this gathering must have been complicated for me, and I will love him for knowing.

I hear Lydia giggle from behind the trees, all nerves and joy, laughter like tinkling bells. The music slows. In Herb's stead, Jake's father, Tim, appears with Lydia to walk her down the grassy aisle, his eyes glistening, cheeks flushed behind his Santa Claus beard. Jake, who is one face with his father minus the bushy white beard, has shed his baseball cap just for today. He waits serenely under the chuppah like a great heron in his bright blue suit and pointy brown leather shoes.

All eyes are on Lydia. Most of all, Jake's. The music stops. Time stops. My throat catches as I watch Tim hand over my daughter to his son. When they exchange vows and rings, fashioned from the melted-down gold of the ring I had slipped on Herb's finger forty-four years ago, I can hardly breathe. The flesh on my bare arms breaks into goosebumps. I pull away from John, shudder, and hug myself. Then I turn and look up into his eyes, shining with benevolence. I exhale and shimmy closer to his warm jacket. It feels like silk.

Now, newlyweds blessed, the wine glass smashed, we recess along the grassy aisle amid smiles and applause, scattering across the lawn and up the hill to the twinkling fairy-lit tent for dinner and dancing. There it all is: the tiny lights in mason jars, the succulents, and the gluten-free carrot cake for 120 guests. As dusk falls, the fairy lights brighten. Each of the twelve tables is adorned with garlands of ivy, its centerpiece a framed reproduction of a botanical rendering of a single herb: sage, thyme, oregano, anise, tarragon, basil, dill, caraway, garlic, mint, parsley, or rosemary. Lydia had found these prints at the Free Library of Philadelphia and obtained permission to copy them. Her father, Herb, is on every table, bathed in a palette of sage green, pale pink, and white.

As mother of the bride, I have been asked to speak. I stride confidently towards the microphone, masking the unsteadiness within. "Let's take a moment to remember Lydia's dad, Herb, who would have given anything to be here tonight. He was cheated of this moment." I stop and look around at the faces in the room, at Herb's brother, the nieces and nephews, the aunts and uncles, the cousins and lifelong friends, and my son, Dan. "Actually," I say, "Herb is right here, among us."

*

From the first to the last dance, John is right here among us, too, reaching for my hand. No one dances like Herb, but John has his own sureness and Latin fluidity; he moves gracefully, feels the music in his hips and shoulders, and I find him easy to follow. I know he is bone tired from deadlines at work, yet he continues. I love him even more for keeping up with all the wildness I had promised my daughter weeks before when she and Jake compiled their wedding playlist, choosing each song with great deliberation.

In her father's honor, Lydia has included "Twist and Shout," Herb's favorite, and "Jeremiah was a Bullfrog," his bedtime song. Dan and I would indeed dance wildly, just as Herb would have, snapping his fingers, moving his feet rhythmically from side to side in what the kids called "the dad-two-step," twirling me around three times: to the left, to the right, and back again, singing in his tremulous *basso profundo*, mouth wide open.

One hour into the dancing, I hear the opening notes to "Jeremiah was a Bullfrog." I let go of John and run to my children. We grab one another in a group hug, jumping and spinning and laughing and crying and singing. *Joy to the fishes in the deep blue sea / Joy to you and me!* John steps aside and watches, perhaps appreciating the respite. The same with "Twist and Shout." We are whirling dervishes. I kick up my legs. John smiles from the periphery. *Shake it, shake it, shake it up, baby, now shake it up, baby / twist and shout / twist, and shout!*

Three hours later, John's custom monogrammed shirt is soaked, his face flushed. Loosening his tie, he removes his jacket and hangs it on the back of his chair. We move slowly now. On the dance floor, we sway in a standing embrace. I relax into his arms, my grateful, tired head on his damp shoulder. My plus one, my last dance.

My Dearest Love, Herb:

Geese mate for life, and so did we. Three days ago, your Lydia became Mrs. Clark. It was excruciating to me that you weren't at the wedding. Wrong. Cruel. Unfair. How could there be such beauty and agony under one big white tent?

But oh, the beauty. Lydia and Jake organized their wedding down to the minutest detail. There were *twenty-five* Mandells there—all connected to you, remembering you. We raised our glasses to you.

The moment of greatest beauty for me was yesterday when a thank you note from Lydia arrived in the mail. It was for *us*, really. "Thank you for being Mommy and Daddy," she wrote. "I know that wasn't easy." Then she cut to the chase: "When I worry about all the *what ifs* with Jake, I know, after having watched you and Dad, that all will be okay. I am ready to do the work, to find the jewels in our marriage."

We did that, baby. We showed our daughter how it is done. Years ago, you exhorted Lydia to find a man who would cherish her. She has. And now the work begins.

What was our work, my love? Of all the things you might have told me the night before you died, pulling me close, speaking in that hoarse whisper with such effort and urgency, you said, "I just can't believe how far we've come together and how much you have grown." As if, at that moment, I was finally graduating into adulthood in a sea of beeping monitors. I brought my lips as close to your feverish face as I dared and whispered back, each word elongated by my breath on the exhale: *We. Had. So. Much.* You smiled. It would be the last time I made you smile. What you may not have noticed, and nor did I: Dan was standing two feet away, listening intently. Later, he would say to me, "That's what I want. I want *that*. To be able to say on my deathbed what Dad said to you, to feel that way about a woman." We did that, baby! We showed our son how it is done. As I write this, Dan is still searching for the one. He will find her.

From the time Dan squirmed his way into our lives, followed by his sister, the two of them watched our every move as we fought over how to raise them. We squabbled like the geese in our backyard, who mated and nested around the pond, flanked by our resident mallard ducks, a cacophony of quacking and honking, fluff, and feather. "Baby geeeeeee," Dan squealed with delight as he lumbered after the peeping, downy, yellow hatchlings following their mother around our yard. Within weeks, they were fully feathered, befouling our property along with their inseparable parents. We couldn't walk from the driveway to the front door without stepping in their gooey mess. "Flying bags of shit," you called them. So beautiful in perfect flight formation, swooping, gliding, and landing on the water, until they denuded our grass and covered it in excrement. We loved-hated those backyard honkers who arrived each February 7th like clockwork, always the same couple, ready to nest. You tried shooing them away with a broom, but, hissing and squawking, the mother goose attacked you, grabbing the cuff of your pant leg in her beak as you tried to run away. You tried firing a pellet gun from the upstairs bathroom window to "incentivize" them to find someone else's pond. They honked and stayed put.

One day, a big red fox came out of our woods and ate our mother goose and her warm, gestating eggs for dinner. You found her goose feathers under a stand of evergreens behind the split rail fence near her nest, you told me. You know all too well how her mate stayed for days, tearing at our hearts as he honked forlornly, swimming back and forth, searching the edges of the pond. Here's what you don't know. After you died, I became that goose. Gray and lifeless. Disoriented. Searching.

Alone in our house, for two years, I wandered around looking for you, staring at the empty seat at the kitchen table, in the dining room, your favorite chair for watching TV, your side of the bed.

An autumn romance has begun for me and John, eight years my senior. A burst of light and color just before the leaves turn to dust, becoming one with the earth. I have colors yet, baby, a vibrance I didn't know I still had, waiting to enter upon the scene. Before the harvest comes.

Remember how, at the beach on a cloudy day, the ocean was gray and then sparkling blue when the sun came out? People do that for one another, evoke color with light.

The wedding is behind me now. I slept the sleep of the dead last night. I dreamt you were back, alive and well, young and vibrant, sleeping in my guest room here at The Plaza with John emerging from my bedroom and encountering you in the hallway. In the dream, I was paralyzed, torn. But. You. Are. Gone.

Tomorrow is Yom Kippur. When we attend Kol Nidrei services tonight, John will wear your *tallis* and *yarmulke*—the first time in three years they are coming out of their bag next to the moth balls since you last wore them in October 2015. I don't know how you would feel about that. I can tell you I long for the closeness I once felt standing by your side all day at High Holy Day services, that blessed pause from our impossibly busy lives. The *yarmulke*, which I carefully clipped to your thinning, curly, white comb-over, still smells like you. Tonight, I will clip the *yarmulke* to John's curly white hair and lay your *tallis* across his broad shoulders. He says he is honored to wear your sacred garments. He will breathe new life into them.

We did the hard work, baby, while our children watched. Do you know what is really the hardest job I ever had to do? Not marriage (hard). Not child-rearing (harder). Not becoming an adult (hardest). Not even having to be "Mommy and Daddy" at Lydia's wedding. It is letting you go.

What Mess?

I am dust settling among the detritus of John's life. How hard will it be for me to settle for all this and his long, circuitous backstory, too? Autumn romance with a messy guy who's had his share of devastating breakups, who yearns at this eleventh hour to get it right with the right woman. I have found a new man who cherishes me. Like Lydia after her wedding, am I ready to do the work? Again?

John has fallen asleep. I sit in his Princeton sleigh bed purchased by one of my more affluent predecessor girlfriends, taking inventory of his room, the voluminous "stuff" of his life, so randomly strewn. Sleeping John smells like toothpaste. I think he eats the stuff. He buys it in bulk. Boxes piled up around his bathroom sink with used-up pens and old toothbrushes. In the corner is an ab-cruncher that I've never seen him use. On his bedside table sit Western-themed Native American murder mysteries and the thousand-page tome, *Surveillance Capitalism*, next to a photo of us in Prague and flexible tubes with a mask for a CPAP machine he never uses. I close my eyes and see my apartment. Sparse, uncluttered, no more than one painting on each wall. I see my few books neatly lined up on my only bookshelf, the kitchen counters clean, and dishes put away. A single tube of toothpaste by my bathroom sink. I open my eyes and see John, a picture of contentment surrounded by clutter. I think of my favorite line from *Fiddler on the Roof*: "A fish can fall in love with a bird, but where will they make their home?"

I lay a hand on his chest and watch it rise and fall, white curls escaping from the V of his T-shirt. I hold him in my heart, his chamber adjoining Herb's. My heart is full of them both. It is dark outside now. John snores.

Earlier on this Friday evening, John sweetly offered to hang up my coat, appearing with a wire hanger, a bit twisted and bent but still functional. I thanked him and wondered where the coat would go, knowing that the closets, all of them, are crammed to bursting. I watched him, so comfortable and at home curled up on his cat-hair-covered, cat-claw-destroyed couch with Hamza purring in his lap, *Washington Week* on the TV, and he alternately attending to the TV and reading a student's term paper. The amount of reading material around his house, in every room, on every surface, is mountainous. One person couldn't possibly read it all. Meanwhile, he is planning his next purchase—a maroon turtleneck to complete the heather-sweater ensemble. Dapper John.

*

"Breakfast with Bach" wafts in from the living room. Sumptuous cello plays on Saturday morning's *Classical Coffeehouse*, now a shared ritual. John still sleeps. I sit at his kitchen island, having pushed aside the piles of mail, coupons, *The New York Times*, cookbooks, pens, cat treats, lint rollers, pills, batteries, loose change, paperclips, trivets, bubble wrap, day timers, and lip balm, just to create a spot for me to set down this journal and write. Hamza meows on and off my lap, his sharp nails digging into my thighs, purring, clawing, and shedding. John does not know how long the curdled milk has been in his fridge. I drink chai tea with half and half, which I brought from home. The tea is warm, and the Bach is beautiful, but I have cat hair in my mouth.

8 a.m. John's clocks say 8:11. It's his little quirk to help him not be late for things, a game he plays with clocks. John

has just emerged and, taking two bowls out of the dishwasher, has put cat food in each. I love watching him feed the cats: his voice purrs when he calls their names.

Now I read John my inventory of his kitchen island, noting a certain not-going-together randomness. Stuff with its own inscrutable logic, a theme recurring as in a symphony, perhaps by John Cage, which repeats itself on his bathroom sink, bedside tables, dining room table, coffee table, chairs, closets, drawers: things that don't go together but just wound up there together. Like toothpaste, pens, and screwdrivers.

But I have this second chance at being loved. By a guy who has been telling me since Prague that he wants to spend the rest of his life with me. By a guy who makes every day an adventure, who teaches me something new, makes me laugh. To have all that and be focused on clutter and cat hair? Perhaps it is I who has the messier mind. *I can settle*, I think, *like dust settles*. I did it once, with my move to The Plaza, declaring, *never again!* And now I say, *look again, think again, begin again.*

Last weekend, John and I sat together in my tidy apartment, across from one another at my uncluttered dining room table. He was reading *The New York Times Book Review*, and I was writing. We both wore our flannel PJs, like an old married couple. How lovely to have him right by my side, the exhaustion of widowhood in the rearview mirror at last.

Now I glimpse the future and wonder, what is it that John, in the end, will have the hardest time giving up? Tennis and skiing? What will he do when the body says *no more*? "I will ski indefinitely," he said last night, delighted with his new streamlined skis and perfect-for-his-feet custom-fit Spiderman boots.

"Tomorrow is trash day," John tells me this morning, his kitchen waste basket overflowing.

"What if?" I say, "what if every week when you put out your trash, you fill one additional can with some of this mess around your house just left to accumulate rust, dust, mold, and cat hair?"

"What mess?" he says.

*

Today, on this lovely May morning, I have taken my coffee out onto the balcony. I breathe in the perfume of lilacs and peonies, Mom's favorites. She would have turned ninety this month, having died nearly a year ago. Yesterday, I called the cemetery where Mom is buried to plan the setting of her headstone, her "unveiling." I remembered that there was a vacant plot next to hers. It hit me: I want to be with her. I called the cemetery back and reserved the plot.

"John," I say when he appears, coffee cup in hand, on this last day of our weekend together, "I am going to be buried next to Bobbie at Mt. Sinai Cemetery near the Tacony–Palmyra Bridge."

John furrows his forehead and raises a bushy white eyebrow.

"I was hoping we could find a way to be together in the hereafter," he says. It catches me by surprise.

"Co-mingle our ashes?" I ask, "We don't even live together!"

It hits me again: I know where I am going for eternity, but right now, I want to live with John and not just on the weekends.

My Dearest Love, John:

I just grinned at you. You raised an eyebrow. "I'm very suspicious of your Cheshire Cat grin," you said. I am grinning because I am sitting inches away across the table from you, writing a love letter instead of talking to you. I am grinning because I just wrote and read you a rant about your messy house, and, raising both eyebrows this time, you said, "I am feeling semi-scathed." I am grinning because when I told you cilantro chelates heavy metals, you said, "I didn't know we've gotten into the chelation stage of our relationship." I am grinning because every time I look at you with what you call my "gimlet eye," you ask, "Why are you looking at me in that tone of voice?" I am grinning because I am thinking, *I could stay with this crinkly-eyed professor with his bushy white eyebrows for the rest of my days.*

What is it with me and erudite, tender-hearted, uproariously funny men? Men of such integrity they don't know how to say anything but the truth, ever. It's all in your eyes.

Last weekend, you dusted off some iconic Pollock family photos for me, and I saw you as a one-year-old, an eighteen-month-old, a twenty-one-year-old, a thirty-six-year-old. The face matured as faces do, but the one constant since age one was your eyes: clear, penetrating. Windows on your soul. Windows on your probing, searching, restless mind that I suspect never sleeps. The light in your eyes burns as I watch from across the table, flashing, darting back and forth, partly concealed under your long-haired, unkempt eyebrows, as your outsized brain formulates a thought, retrieves a memory, contrives stories you tirelessly tweak and retell as your unfolding life narrative.

Your foundation story, which any woman would find beguiling: a three-year-old boy and his grandmother, Flora. An artist who read you Dickens and Shakespeare and took you to museums, ballet, and opera—planting seeds of culture that took root for a lifetime, conferring the sensibilities of a poet and a longing to be a college professor before you knew how to read. I have imagined you relating that charming story of your precocity to every woman you ever met but not to the men you "talk trash" to and persistently outlast on the tennis courts. You play to win. I love a man with boundaries.

You had a gifted first-grade teacher who, when you still could not read, told your worried mother, "Leave him to me. He'll learn." Once you did, there was no stopping you. No one I know has ever read as voraciously as you (except, perhaps, Herb). "I have always lived vicariously through books," you told me the other night as if it were an epiphany.

Your commonalities with Herb fascinate us both. The *basso profundo* singing voice. The broken noses forever askew—in your case, from wrestling in the bathroom with your younger brother, Craig, who died when you were twenty-nine. The knowing what you were going to grow up to be practically from birth. The crooked teeth—no money for orthodonture (except for the girls). Both Ivy League scholarship kids, self-made, workaholic, driven, and insecure about money. Encyclopedic minds, near-perfect recall, and endlessly curious about absolutely everything.

You were deeply humbled at Swarthmore. After your ascent into stardom at Golden High School as a scholar-athlete-tennis-star-champion-debater, you were gut-punched by the college's academic demands as well as the social and intellectual sophistication of your East Coast, often Jewish friends. There was humility and perseverance in your resilience at Swarthmore, nurtured by kind classmates and attentive deans, and by a lifetime of being "the boy from somewhere else" as your parents moved back and forth from Tacoma to Dallas to the California Bay Area to Alabama and then Colorado. Having to swim once again in a different pond at Swarthmore, later at Stanford, and finally on the East Coast as a professor, reinventing yourself to make new friends was already your default strategy. You have never, you told me, stopped longing to be part of a community. You envy me, you say, I who never left Philadelphia. You envy my strong synagogue ties and join us for Torah Study every Saturday. You say, quoting Levi-Strauss, "It's the retelling of our communal story that strengthens the bonds of membership in a community." Meanwhile, I envy you, my citizen of the world who, chameleon-like, adapts to his surroundings.

"Somewhere else" for you, most of all, is Colorado, where riding horses and skiing were what you and all the kids did many days after school. Last summer, you took me home, where the buffalo roam—literally—to Lookout Mountain and Buffalo Bill's grave, where you worked all summer at age sixteen for eighty cents an hour, persuading the children of tourists to ask their parents to buy them cowboy hats and papoose dolls. You took me to the swimming pool where you worked as a lifeguard after high school, where, had I been there as a ten-year-old, crush-besotted preteen, you, from your exalted perch on the lifeguard stand, would have swatted me away like a fly. We hiked to "Lion Rock," a precipice overlooking the Continental Divide where you and your sister recently scattered your parents' ashes. A sacred pilgrimage for you; for me, an essential expedition without which I never could have claimed to know you.

Sometimes, we stop in mid-conversation when beautiful music plays on the radio, our talk a mundane intrusion upon the holiness of sound. You hold up your hand like a traffic cop when the music ends. Our silence must persist until the announcer tells us what we just heard: composer, artist, what, where, when, solidly anchored in its national, ethnic, linguistic, or cultural context, time, and place. I indulge your "need to know," though for me, the evocative beauty is enough. You want more: the specifics must land in the Rolodex of your capacious brain, where all facts and figures are sorted and stored. Ready for retrieval next time.

We are fusing together, you and I, becoming one. Music is often our wordless medium, we who traffic in words. We are transitioning from the effort of courtship, which requires a leap of faith, into something else. Something enduring.

Eight years my senior, you are aging backward, you tell me, because you are in love. You are the only one "your age" among your tennis buddies, you say, who is not retired. There will always be work, you say, honorable work, and never enough time. You refuse to die, as you believe your father did, "with the music still inside you."

Your squamous cell carcinoma on the right side of your tongue is back, you said last night, according to a recent biopsy. "I've had a good run," you said. "It's been nine years since my last surgery." You told me early on that a quarter of your tongue was already missing, that the cancer would recur. Last summer, during our travels out West, you said once or twice, "My tongue feels funny. I will have it checked out back home."

I am no stranger to men who look death right in the eye, men who accept their fate with steely resolve and quiet equanimity. I will accompany you next week to Jefferson for your tongue resection. You are already anxious about writing and delivering a keynote in Beijing three weeks after the surgery. You wonder if you will be able to speak coherently, not just in Beijing, but ever.

Lying in recovery in the hospital with me by your side, you will say, loopy from the anesthesia, "This is the first time I truly feel like you could be my wife." We will rejoice that you can still speak, even with a skin graft over the surgical site. You will drift off to sleep with that faint smile I love, as I promise not to leave until you have fallen asleep. I will drive you home the next morning, stopping at Reading Terminal Market for rum raisin ice cream, and nurse you back to health in my apartment for eleven days, feeding you a cornucopia of pureed foods as you struggle, in pain, to swallow, to speak. Your tongue will hemorrhage all over my bed. It will heal, and I've got Clorox.

You will recover just in time to make the arduous journey to China. There, you will hobnob with some of the most distinguished colleagues in your field, returning home with all kinds of new ideas for future collaborations for your next book, all the while keeping alive the flames of passion with your girl. More than a girlfriend. I am becoming something else. Like a wife, but not a wife. I know I am your one and only, as you are mine.

Sometimes, I feel like you are the one who is eight years younger. Especially last winter when you texted me from your ski trip to Deer Valley, hitting the slopes with your best friend, Rick:

We just had one of the finest days of skiing I can ever remember. The conditions were perfect: light powder on a packed base, the best Rocky Mountain sky imaginable. The brightest sun, and my magical new skis. Rick has new magic skis as well, and we swooped and dove and soared like fledgling birds eager to try out their newfound ability to fly. We were on fire!

And the rich, reassuring company of old friends is a special blessing. With that, and having found the love of my life, I am about as close to heaven as any mortal is allowed to go.

I woke up the next morning to a photo you sent of you and Rick having dinner in a "yurt." I love that photo so much. You and Rick look like twins. You are both smiling with tiredness after a day on the slopes. The photo speaks to friendship, fierce friendship. Rick could be your stand-in for your lost brother, Craig; you regard all your male friends as brothers.

You would save their lives if you had to. Two men in a yurt with a shared love of skiing, tennis, and The College of New Jersey. Two men who are exactly where they want to be at that moment in time, happy-tired, having dinner together after a day of skiing, in a yurt where time stands still.

Where has the time gone? I have been scribbling away for hours here at my dining room table. You have gone off to get dressed for your big teaching day. You have just appeared in your signature khaki trousers, sexy camel's hair sport jacket, and lavender striped shirt, custom made and monogrammed on the sleeve—oh, how you scrutinized and selected, with such care, the purple threads and lettering for that monogram. My beloved peacock in a cowboy hat. Off to school you go. Your students have no idea what they are in for today.

Love in the Time
of Coronavirus

I have absolutely no idea on March 20, 2020, as the world shuts down around us, that John will show up at my Plaza apartment with two roller bags and stay for *two years*. It has been over two years since we met and took that pretend honeymoon in Prague, and now, finally, we are forced to live together in my sparse thousand-square-foot two-bedroom den. I am delighted to have him there with me. I still see no reason to get married, but playing married will be lovely, I think.

At first, at The Plaza, I couldn't stop crying. I hated the long, windowless hallway and having to take an elevator up and down from my sixth-floor apartment to go anywhere. I missed my capacious, light-filled home and being able to walk outside to lie in my hammock by the pond.

I met my closest Plaza neighbor the first day, a knock at my door. "Hi, I'm Diana. I live across the hall." She handed me a plate of warm, just-baked chocolate chip cookies. "Welcome to the sixth floor. We think this is the best floor in the building because the nicest people live here." Diana, I would learn, was a widow, not unlike eighty percent of The Plaza's residents. I was hardly unique, just twenty years younger than most. Diana walked the halls daily for exercise, logging in her steps and catching up on everyone's news. Down by the trash chute, next to the elevators, we all encountered one another with a smile, a wave. By the time I met John, I was enjoying apartment living and my kind neighbors. Even better, I loved it when John tipped his cowboy hat to the ladies of the sixth floor on his way to and from my apartment.

Now, when I stand in my tiny kitchen for hours slicing and dicing, John appears out of nowhere and kisses the back of my neck.

Now, he sits beside me when I curl up with Marge Piercy's *The Hunger Moon*, which he ordered for me on Amazon, and I can smell his toothpaste. "Read it aloud," he says. Resting my feet on his lap, watching his face as I read, I listen for the *whoof*, that little shudder of amazement which bubbles up from his throat whenever a verse touches him. He strokes the tops of my feet, eyes closed.

Now, in the evenings, he sits in his favorite dark green leather chair and reads his beloved Western-themed novels. "It's how I relax," he says. The softness in his face, the shine in his eyes tracking the words on the page, the bemused curl of his lips say: *I am in my happy place.* He does not hear me walk into the room. His contentment calms me.

*

Covid, though, terrifies me more each day: face masks, latex gloves, sanitizing, social distancing, all in the interest of staying well. So much suffering everywhere. I worry about running out of food and hair dye. I learned today that pet adoptions are up.

"As my hair gets longer, it will get curly," John says.

I've always liked poodles.

I learn how to cut his curly hair. And my own, in the mirror, cutting backward, making mistakes—a gouge here and there. *Hair grows back.*

"Love in the time of coronavirus," John says.

It astonishes me to have so quickly adapted to our new life. I secretly enjoy not having to exercise as much as I used to. I adore our Passover-for-two without our bantering children—the way we focus on reading the Haggadah and savoring the retelling of its stories. John inhales the vats of charoset I made just for us—chopped apples, walnuts, red wine, cinnamon, and honey—his favorite Passover food. Unrushed, we linger over what John calls "sacred texts" from Exodus that chronicle the liberation of the Jews from slavery in Egypt. John looks, as he does, for the through line that connects ancient history with current events. We ponder the oppression of other peoples in other places and times, including our own. We munch on charoset long into the early spring evening.

*

Spring in Covid lockdown.

John sleeps.

I have moved to the other end of my dining room table as I write to look out the balcony doors into the light of morning. Eggshell-blue sky. Rooftops, treetops sun-drenched, budding trees announcing themselves, adorned in pale green, soft pastels bathed in light. Music pours forth from the kitchen and light from the doors. Morning light, morning music, morning blessings. Shabbat, fourth day of Passover. Tomorrow, Easter. Yesterday, we listened to Bach's "St. Matthew Passion."

John appears in his madras underwear as a Yiddish song from 1943 plays on the radio: "Birds are snoozing in the branches." This, written in the middle of World War II.

Out in the world, says NPR, more coronavirus is again plaguing China, believed to be brought there by Chinese nationals returning from Russia, prompting the closure of the Chinese-Russian border. Meanwhile, fossil fuel consumption is way down worldwide. There is now an oversupply (no one is driving or flying), so this has put a hold on price wars between oil-producing nations. This has also reduced air pollution globally by twenty percent.

Spring comes regardless. Like Anne Frank was confined to an attic, a girl who, over the span of her confinement, developed from a pre-teen into a full-blown adolescent, we too continue our development: aging and growing, the arc of our lives continuing uninterrupted as the trees keep budding and opening into leaf outside, heedless of the devastation wrought by a pandemic.

I have not felt so content in a long time as I did this morning, awakening by John's side. I wrapped my arms and my body around him as I often do, wondering if he knew I was there, thinking even if he didn't know, he *knew*. Our bodies communicate: magnets drawn, slammed together by force of attraction and longing for connection—irresistible, inseparable, bound together. On Shabbat and every day. In the time of coronavirus, and always. Peggy and John. Completing one another. Bodies intertwined; souls connected.

Shabbat Shalom.

Happy Passover.

Happy Easter.

Happy spring.

*

We binge on *Outlander*, the "Skye Boat Song" ringing in our ears as we drift off to sleep each night. I feel a little cheap relying on gorgeous Jamie and Claire for our love story script. They fire up our sex life. Do we imagine we look like them, too? Maybe forty years ago. We can pretend.

"Let's summon central casting to dress us up like eighteenth-century Scottish aristocracy: corsets for me, blousy white shirts for you," I say to John. He smiles. He loves dressing up. He calls clothes his "costume." Too bad we have nowhere to go, my peacock in a cowboy hat.

Other than food and Netflix, we stop consuming most commodities like gasoline and jet fuel. But maybe food and

Netflix are all we need. Not quite. John still has a full-time job teaching college even though his campus is shut down and his students have been sent home. He and his students and folks everywhere are taking a crash course on how to use Zoom. He has scanned all his students' papers so they can see his edits on "share screen." He is figuring out how to make a virtual background and set up breakout "rooms" for class discussion. A month ago, we hadn't heard of Zoom. Now, it's a lifeline for connection with the entire outside world. "I love eavesdropping when you are teaching your students," I tell John. When I hear his ho-ho-ho belly laugh erupt through the thin walls of my apartment, it warms me all over.

I'm learning to use Zoom, too, having been asked by my boss to teach yoga at the studio where I worked before lockdown. Now I sit on my dining room floor staring at women in tiny "gallery view" squares who are trying to follow my poses, my laptop on the floor next to me. I fuss with the lighting and camera angle. It's a theatrical production! I send the video recordings to my boss, who archives and sells them. Now I know what I look like teaching, what my voice sounds like—it is soothing, I think. Sometimes, when John is not teaching, he pulls up a chair and joins my yoga practice in the dining room, grunting offscreen, sniggering when I tell my all-female class, "Tighten your vaginal muscles."

*

Spring lockdown rolls into summer. I want to be with him all the time. Confined to a thousand square feet, I concoct our favorite meals—spinach, bacon, beet, and goat cheese salad. I savor these summer mornings and evenings out on the balcony, even with the noise of all the delivery trucks. We joke about the Coca-Cola eighteen-wheeler that seems to arrive like clockwork every evening around sunset, pulling up to the ACME loading dock.

He is negotiating terms for his new book, *Covid in International Media*, for which he will be senior editor. It will occupy him all summer and beyond. This work excites him, animates him, especially cultivating international connections. My citizen of the world, confined to the sixth floor of a high-rise. He tells me often that being with me gets his creative juices going, fires up his intellectual curiosity. This morning, in the early quiet, I think of myself as his muse here in Covid lockdown. Someday soon, I will well up when he tells me he is dedicating his book to me: "to Peggy, who brightens every day." And then again, when he publishes a second book, *Covid Communication*, and dedicates that one to me too: "to Peggy, who enriches every relationship." *If only.*

When I tell him that I have decided to transcribe my fourteen journals of handwritten love letters, so much ink on the page from so many Pilot pens, onto my computer, he raises his bushy white eyebrows and crinkles his eyes at me, which makes me want to start right away. He is *my* muse, too! All these summer projects are taking the place of what he and I might have been doing, had planned on doing—like last summer when he took me out West to see where he grew up, and then we flew to Madrid for another international conference, and then to Barcelona. But here we sit. We both journey into the "inner sky" of mind and imagination.

A way of life has ended. And while our trips to beautiful and exotic places were full of challenge, adventure, and discovery, I just don't care that there's been a course correction, because I am blooming in this tiny little garden with Coca-Cola trucks making sunset deliveries.

Who is drinking all that soda?

Truce

At some point, I start picking little fights—his cell phone, the laundry.

"Could there be just two of us at the table when we eat?" I ask him.

"What?" he says.

"Your cell phone. I light the candles, turn on the music, and plate and serve the food. Then, you set that little black rectangle right next to your fork. It vibrates. It lights up. You pick it up. You put it down. I can't compete."

He furrows those bushy white eyebrows.

Finally, the little black rectangle is gone.

Occasionally, he will forget and my greatest rival for his attention again shows up at the table.

*

I scrub the toilets and do the wash, which he never does, no matter how long it keeps piling up.

"John," I wail from inside the small closet where my washer and dryer sit stacked.

"What?"

"You forgot to take those tissues out of your pockets again—there's lint all over my black yoga pants. And everything else."

"Sorry," he says.

The following week, the same.

I still have no idea how we will share a home.

*

The big hurt.

We are walking home from a neighborhood stroll. I can see he is sweating as he removes his cowboy hat and sunglasses and wipes his brow mid-conversation.

"What would it take for us to move in together?" I continue. "Let's face it. I really don't want to move again, and you don't want to downsize and sell your home in Princeton."

"I have set aside the last week in August for cleaning out," he says testily.

"I don't believe you," I say. "I know you will come up with a million projects and distractions to avoid this task. You have already agreed to edit two books on Covid over the summer. Andy rented a house in Ocean City for the last week in August and invited us. I want to go with our bikes and stay until Thursday to avoid the weekend crowds at the shore, especially during Covid. *I want to bike along the ocean. Just once.*" I feel like crying.

"Then I can't join you," he says, voice rising. "That's not enough time for me to work on the garage." Louder: "I was expecting you to stay until Saturday so I could come down at the end of the week." Louder still: "This means I can't come at all." My skin itches, I feel prickles on the back of my neck. I am hot. I am, quite suddenly, seven years old and afraid of this yelling man.

"Now I know why you are still single," I hiss just to shut him up. I sound like my mother. *I wonder if she ever wanted to take back the hurtful words she said to us kids or to our father.* Too late. Regret, a familiar worm in my belly.

John's face goes slack. He looks at the ground.

Upstairs, without looking at one another, we eat our lunch of citrus salad with balsamic vinaigrette and toasted pistachios. The oranges and grapefruit are acid on my tongue, the dressing sour, and the nuts soggy.

"John," I say quietly, putting down my fork, searching for words beyond the hackneyed *I'm sorry.* "I have no idea where that remark came from or why I said it. It's not even true. I have no excuse, no explanation." *And I pledged, before Lydia's wedding, to hold my tongue.*

"What set you off?" he asks in a whisper.

Dare I tell him? That I am still seven years old? That I am my mother? That in an instant, because he yelled, I became this person I did not want to recognize as myself?

"It was your tone, your anger. It scared me, like my parents yelling at each other." He waits, listening.

I begin softly. "The scariest night for me was when, as a seven-year-old, I curled up in my pink flannel pajamas outside my parents' bedroom, my ear glued to the crack under the door. I was there because I wanted to hear them kissing. Instead, I heard fighting. 'You're drunk again,' Mom wailed. 'You are gambling away our money.' He yelled back indistinctly, speech slurred. She shrieked, and I imagined him hitting her. I ran back to my bed, shaking. Next, I heard my father retching and vomiting in the toilet. It was loud because their bathroom and my bedroom shared the same wall. I remember sticking my fingers in my ears. I still do that. Loud noises, especially human ones, have always terrified me."

John falls silent. I watch him, waiting. I truly fear he is going to take his two roller bags and walk out the door, tipping his cowboy hat to Diana for the last time.

I should have known better.

He finishes his citrus salad.

He will yell again, and so will I. And we will forgive.

Covid Comes to the Sixth Floor

Just before the pandemic hit, a new couple about my age moved in down the hall. The wife noticed a bike rack on the back of my car and left a note on my windshield asking if we'd like to go biking with them sometime. "Sure," we said the next time we saw her at the trash chute.

We would never take that bike ride. The tsunami of Covid would fell five of our sixth-floor neighbors in the space of one month, including this woman's husband. I never knew his name. Diana would tell me at the trash chute. "Five people, just on our floor!" she said, double-masked on her morning power walk down our windowless hallway. I could smell her fear, saw it in her eyes as she peered over her mask. The same fear washed over me as I shook my head slowly from side to side. *The nicest people in the building.* Diana turned ninety during Covid, celebrating alone on Zoom with her grandchildren. If anyone passed her in the hallway, she turned and faced the wall. Two doors down, a man living alone expired on his living room floor and was not discovered for three days. Plaza management duct-taped the vent between his apartment and the hallway, taped a do-not-enter sign on his door, and, for an entire week, vented his apartment out his balcony door using a noisy, very powerful exhaust fan. One day in the elevator, observing the two-person-only rule, I found myself with the biker whose husband had just died. I thought of Herb in the

ICU, suffocating, doctors and nurses bustling in and out wearing hazmat gear to protect themselves from Herb's raging pneumococcus infection. Now, one thousand Americans were dying on ventilators every day in complete isolation. "How are you doing?" I said quietly to this woman I barely knew. "Some days are better than others," she sighed. *I know. I know.* The next day, Diana stopped me: "Do you have any idea how lucky you are not to be alone?" *I know. I know.*

Betwixt Sea and Sky

After Covid, there was no turning back. This fish had fallen so hard for the bird (and vice versa) that we just had to find a way to make our home, somewhere betwixt sea and sky, between Pennsylvania and New Jersey, mess be damned.

But where, when, and how?

During Covid, we tiptoed around the question of marriage. My heart filled nearly to bursting one morning when John said, "I knew the day you wrote that first love letter to me last fall that we would always be together." It gave me hope that maybe, finally, we could agree on "what is a life partnership" in the endgame of our lives. I knew John yearned to be married to me, but I gently questioned why anyone our age would marry when we would not be having children or owning property together. After I sold my big house in Wyncote, I vowed never to burden myself again with the physical and financial responsibility of home ownership. It had its place and time in the misty corridors of my achingly beautiful memories of life with Herb and our children. To this day, my heart quickens when I drive down our old street and peek under the mailbox to see if Herb's ashes are still there.

But I've moved on. John, on the other hand, seemed no closer to emptying and selling his house in Princeton than he did three years ago, and it finally dawned on me why. Being married, raising children, and owning the roof over his head was a substantive marker of manhood for John. Just as for Herb, his home was his castle, his fiefdom, his own slice of the world. It's why the kids and I knew the proper place for Herb's ashes was right in our backyard. John was encumbered with a large mortgage that precluded paying rent for a place with me until he could sell his house, yet something was holding him back.

When we finally did move in together, and I covered all the initial expenses so he could continue to pay his mortgage, he would confess that until then, he did not truly believe I wouldn't up and leave him as his wife once did. "Goodness, John, could I possibly have any more skin in the game here?" Only then did he call a realtor and begin in earnest to empty the house in preparation for sale. A large dumpster appeared in his driveway. But first, we had to find a place for the two of us. In Pennsylvania because I insisted, but close to New Jersey because he worked there.

As for marriage, I was sure I would not change my mind. "You know, you've never actually *asked* me to marry you, John," I said one day. "Because you've made clear what the answer would be," he said. Still, I wanted to be asked.

Our three-semester honeymoon in lockdown at The Plaza came to a screeching halt when The College of New Jersey required John, and all faculty, to resume teaching in person on campus. He commuted back and forth from Jenkintown to the college, his face increasingly ashen at the end of each workday. An unsustainable drain on his stamina, I knew, for this uncomplaining, soon-to-be eighty-year-old.

I called my realtor from Berkshire-Hathaway, who referred me to Sharon, an expert on Bucks County rentals. "It's a seller's market right now," she said, "with the housing demand since Covid escalating each day. Don't call me until you are ready to move because anything available today will be gone tomorrow."

"Please show me what you have," I said. It was late September.

"You need," she said, "to be locked and loaded with proof that you are financially qualified, ready to sign a rental agreement at a moment's notice." We scrambled to compile bank statements and tax returns as I moved money out of my savings account into a checking account to prove we had cash to cover three months' rent. They required a letter of recommendation from our current property manager to vouch that we were good tenants. Each evening, we pored over the specs for available properties. *Coming soon! Just listed! No longer available!*

We needed to get out there and look. Sharon arranged a Tuesday morning tour. By ten that morning, we were walking through several of the townhomes we had seen online.

Close to noon, we pulled into a cul-de-sac called Randolph Court to visit an end unit just listed the evening before. Before we even got out of the car, John was smiling more broadly than I'd ever seen him smile. Still outside, he eyed the bay window off the large eat-in-kitchen. "The bird feeders will go here," he said. Inside, his pupils dilated as sunlight streamed in through the stained-glass fan light in the large family room, caddy-corner from the brass fireplace. He noticed the high ceilings, chair rails, baseboard and crown molding in every room, the light on three sides, the burnt-sienna-stained wood floors, and the master bedroom suite with two walk-in closets. He claimed the second bedroom as his study, peering out at the arboretum of mature evergreen and deciduous trees nestled across sweeping lawns visible from every window in the house. I liked it. *John wanted it.*

That night, when I called Sharon to say we were ready to sign the rental agreement for Randolph Court, she said, "The owners, Mark and Laura, have already received five offers."

"Should we even bother?" I asked with a sideways glance at John, suddenly crestfallen.

"You never know," Sharon said. "Sometimes writing a letter helps."

"A letter?" John said, brightening. "They have no idea whom they are dealing with. Write the letter! Write the letter!"

He was jumping up and down. "Maybe they should just have a swimsuit contest and be done with it," I muttered, bleary-eyed from our long day of home-hunting. I started typing.

Dear Mark and Laura:

John and I are delighted to submit a rental application for your lovely home at Randolph Court. You must have really loved living there—it shows in the tasteful touches you added throughout the house.

We, too, treat our homes with TLC, and even in a rental would take care of your place as if we had built it ourselves. I am an immaculate housekeeper—I am descended from a long line of women who always prided themselves in maintaining and cleaning their beautiful homes. Any time I stay somewhere, I leave it nicer than when I found it. That's just me. By the way, I am a certified yoga instructor, and I adore your hardwood floors! I am also a gourmet cook, and my kitchen sparkles like yours.

John is a full-time professor in Public Health and Communications Studies at The College of New Jersey. He is an internationally renowned scholar who has published many books, including two that just came out on global responses to Covid. He longs for light-filled spaces in which to write and, for inspiration, lots of trees and grass to view outside—you must have loved that about your house. We do.

We hope you will accept our application and know you have other interest. (Are you planning a swimsuit contest?) If you choose us as your next tenants, we think you will be glad you did, as we will respect and care for your property as if it were our own. We would be thrilled to meet you.

Sincerely,

Margaret Mandell and John Pollock

I emailed my letter to Sharon at 11:00 p.m. Fifteen minutes later, she replied, "You got the house. It was the letter."

I had just committed us to a November 1st move-in and several months' rent penalty at The Plaza for breaking my lease. I had just reduced John's work commute from sixty to fifteen minutes, moving to a town where I knew absolutely no one—to Siberia (that frozen wasteland, as Tevia says in *Fiddler on the Roof*), I would tell my synagogue friends. I was moving nearly an hour away from Lydia, who had bought a house near Jenkintown so we could see one another. She'd brought us groceries every week during Covid, and I'd fed her backyard chickens when she and Jake went out of town. This marked the end of our mother-daughter *sure, I'll be right over, sweetie* time together and the beginning of something else. A declaration of love for John, I thought, and it felt right despite Lydia's sadness and mine, too. There must be supermarkets and places to teach yoga and parks with beautiful bike trails out there somewhere. There would be.

John was ebullient as we DocuSigned the agreement at midnight. I was prepared, as instructed, to go to the bank at 9:00 a.m. the next day and Fed-Ex a certified check for three months' rent to the owners of Randolph Court to secure our rental agreement.

Tell them about the letter, John would beg every time we got together with friends for months afterward, as we shared our newest foundation story, how we came to jointly occupy our dream house in Newtown, PA. I am a letter writer, but storytelling is in John's DNA, going all the way back to his grandmother, Flora, the one who read Dickens to him at the age of three. "I teach my students to be social scientists," he says often, "when I promise them that together we will find the *story* in the numbers, in the data." John was the one who pushed me to turn my love letters into a story, but this move to Newtown was a prologue to a new chapter in our lives, a chapter whose outcome I could not yet imagine.

Preparing to move yet again, all I could think was, *Oh no, now I have three toilets and five sinks to clean, twenty-one hundred square feet of floor to vacuum, a garage to sweep out, ceiling-to-floor windows to wash, Windex at the ready.* I started driving back and forth between Jenkintown and Newtown with my vacuum cleaner in the back seat of my car. I wanted the floors dust-free before the movers got there. I am indeed descended from a long line of German-Jewish housewives.

But I was so wrong about one thing. I thought I was making this move to please John. In the end, it was I who was the most thrilled to land in this Newtown love nest, enchanted by the morning light, the colorful birds at the feeder, and the dreamy kitchen. A real house again.

"Here's the deal," I said in my most authoritative Joe Biden voice: "You get the floors and the walls for your rugs and artworks; I'm bringing over my furniture from The Plaza. It's all we need." John's home in Princeton was filled with Persian rugs and more art, collected from all over the world, than he had room for. The rugs were magnificent but hard to appreciate in their current location, as they were mostly covered with piles of stuff and cat hair. I sent Maloumian Oriental Carpet Cleaning over to pick up his rugs to be professionally cleaned and delivered to Newtown before the movers arrived.

Giving John the walls was conditioned upon his choosing only his favorite pieces to bring over, being selective. *No clutter allowed.* First, I had to amputate a few more of my limbs, giving away my china and crystal, the last vestiges of Herb's art collection that made it onto the walls of my Plaza apartment, plus a few treasured paintings I had taken from my mom's home after she died. I wept and wept as I delivered them to thrift stores. But I was wrong again: I didn't need them anymore. I thanked them for their service and felt strangely free.

I would grow to adore John's collection of works from Africa, Japan, China, Mexico, and New Mexico as if they had just become mine. The folk art, the Lascaux horses, vases, the porcelain statuettes, even the silly winged lions, those Nepalese hearth guardians he stuck under the fireplace when I wasn't looking. "Please," I said to John more than once, "don't bring anything into this house unless you've cleaned it first."

I feigned disgruntlement when the stuff came in caked with dust and was, in some instances, moldy or water-damaged from long stints in John's basement or garage. There are some things John just does not see, and dirt is one of them. I ran around with rags and Windex, soap, and water, even screwdrivers to take apart some of the frames when the glass was broken and needed to be replaced.

What John does see is beauty. "It's so good to appreciate this artwork all over again, here in *our* home," he said, beaming. He scrutinized his pieces of art, noting their colorful, whimsical, meticulous detail. He retold the stories of their acquisition while hammering picture hooks into the walls, a leveler in one hand and a yardstick in the other. Two paintings by his grandmother, Flora, and several from her collection brought over from China, where John's mother was born, would adorn our new living room and dining room walls.

Wide-eyed and full of wonder, John also sees the birds who visit each morning: chickadee, downy woodpecker, slate-colored junco, purple finch and goldfinch, English sparrow, cardinal, white-breasted nuthatch, tufted titmouse, blue jay, and dove. He never tires of refilling the bird feeders and smiling his grateful grin with each new fine-feathered arrival. I never tire of watching his face when the birds come.

What mess?

We had signed a two-year lease, already certain that we would renew it for two more years, maybe four. We had no idea that fate had other plans for us. We were certain we were home.

A Kitchen Tale

My mother bent over the oven with her turkey baster, her face flushed, blue-and-white striped apron tied in a bow. It would be my brother Larry's job to carve once he was old enough. "He has the hands of a surgeon," she said. A potholder in her left hand to steady the pan, she used her right hand to pump the rubber bulb, squirting golden liquid over sizzling skin. My nostrils flared with pleasure long before I could understand words like *poultry seasoning* or *sage, rosemary*, or *thyme*. I wanted to wear that apron and squirt pan juices all over the breasts and legs of that plump, thirsty bird, making it glow and filling the house with an aroma that could only mean one thing: Thanksgiving. I understood before I had words that cooking used heat to change the color, smell, taste, and texture of food. I wanted to cook, to feed, to nurture, to transform by cutting, chopping, mixing, and heating.

Once, when I was seven, I decided to invite all the neighborhood kids for lunch without asking my mother, who was very busy corralling my active younger brothers. It was going to be my first party: grilled cheese sandwiches. I lined up twelve Wonder bread slices along the red Formica kitchen table and placed a square of American cheese on top of each one. They looked so pretty: a square on top of a square! Mom came in and scowled, "What are you doing?" "I'm having a party," I said and named all the children who were coming. "No, you are not," she said and handed me the phone. "Call them now." I couldn't stop crying. I couldn't even explain why suddenly there was no party. Worse, I had to speak mostly to their mothers. *I just wanted to have a party.*

I'd always want to have a party, want to cook: first, for my brothers when I babysat and then for my friends in college, then for Herb's extended family and our children, then for John. Steadfast, implacable me, shaped by that longing planted deep inside me each year, one Thanksgiving after another, watching my mother with her turkey baster.

Today, roasting and basting, my nose knows when the meat is done; I know by the color and tautness of the skin, the sound of the sizzle. I bend towards the hot oven, face flushed, and feel there are two of us lifting the heavy pan, Mom and me. Now, I cook twenty-one meals a week for John, each one a new creation, a transformation.

I cooked my first-ever meal for Herb in my small High-Rise East apartment at Penn just after we met. I made chicken— *poulet à l'orange*, I called it, to make it sound fancy. When he cut into it, I could see it was still bloody. He seemed not to notice. I felt his unconditional love for me start to blossom that night. *Love me, love my food.*

At one point, it happened: it was my turn to take over the making of Thanksgiving dinner. Lydia was in college, and I was substituting arrowroot for flour to thicken the giblet gravy, having purged my entire kitchen of gluten after her Celiac diagnosis. My mother, thrilled to show up and be served, always had double helpings of mashed potato pie, her favorite comfort food. Everyone else's, too.

But I was nervous. I have always been nervous about doing this thing that I love—cooking for those who are dear to me. It's like singing in front of an audience. You want to know with certainty that it's going to be good, but you never know what might go wrong, no matter how hard you try.

This year's Thanksgiving is no different. Except that I want it to be Norman Rockwell.

It's my turn because, for the past two years during Covid,

Lydia had hosted Thanksgiving dinner, first in her cozy back-yard under a heat lamp Dan and I purchased for the occasion before there were vaccines, and then in her dining room after we all got boosted. I could see the cooking had exhausted her. "How would you like a year off?" I'd asked her in September, and she nearly wept with relief. In October, she asked, "Do you know what you're making?"

"Of course," I said.

"Of course," she said. Three peas in a pod: Lydia, my mother, and me. Planners all.

*

The kitchen in this rented townhouse is a cook's dream. A farm sink so big you can wash the biggest stock pot and twelve-inch cast-iron skillet at the same time. A reliable gas range with one big oven, four burners, and a microwave. Ample counter space with room for my Cuisinart (without which there would be no mashed potato pie, cranberry orange chutney with ginger and raw honey, or julienne strips of carrot and zucchini for my cucumber-avocado slaw) and a small toaster oven (for toasting almonds at the last minute to sprinkle on the must-be-tender-crisp green beans with shiitake mushrooms).

Best of all, this is a huge eat-in kitchen with a bay window that now houses John's parents' cherry dining room table from his childhood home in Colorado. John swears he still can see the Continental Divide whenever he sits here. On weekends, we linger over coffee, reading *The New York Times*, and talking about our future together. Birds titter on the feeders my bird-obsessed professor had installed just outside the window, as he offers up a litany of sightings: "A goldfinch! A female cardinal! A tufted titmouse! A downy woodpecker!"

Here at John's childhood table, I set up the Thanksgiving buffet. I busy myself with magic markers, writing labels for each dish, and listing the ingredients (for Lydia) as my mother always had.

Don't Google ways-to-cook-a-Thanksgiving-turkey unless you want to get lost in a rabbit hole. Over the years, I have tried everything. High heat. Low heat. Brining. Smoking on a grill. With and without basting. Wrapped in foil. Injecting butter under the skin. Miscalculating cooking time while the green beans got soggy. Dry, dry, dry. It turns out: turkey *is* dry. The issue is in the tissue.

This year, I know what to do. Make everything in advance; *be prepared.* Make everything you know how to make, tried and true. Above all, the turkey. Just roast it, cavity stuffed with aromatic herbs, a lemon, and an onion. The day before. Let it take as long as it wants to reach an internal temperature of 165. Let it sit, and then carve everything off the bone (except the drumsticks) and refrigerate it covered in a good, rich broth, mixed with the pan drippings. Reheat in the oven just before serving and pour off the broth for tender, juicy, flavorful meat, and voila! There it is on John's parents' old dining room table, flanked by a spinach-broccoli souffle, oven-roasted sweet potatoes, cranberry chutney, cornbread with room temperature grass-fed cultured butter, Lydia's stuffing, and sizzling mashed potato pie. Mushroom gravy simmering on the stove top next to the sauteed green beans amandine. A crock pot on the kitchen table filled with smoked brisket in case the turkey runs out. It won't, but Jake loves brisket. It is for him. Everything is perfect. Everything is ready. I am relaxed and confident. My last Thanksgiving dinner in a house.

As our extended family starts arriving, John keeps beaming. "Our kids really like each other," he whispers. He stands to the side and watches, picking up snitches of banter among the kids in the living room, then meanders back to the kitchen, meeting my gaze, eyes shining.

Lydia and Jake, four years married and settled into their own house in Elkins Park with six hens a-laying in their backyard, are here with their dog, Nala, so they won't need to run home to walk her. My sweet granddoggy is all curled up on her portable bed, making herself at home on my living room rug. Since Covid and multiple work-from-home job changes, Lydia works long hours selling software services remotely. Her laughter still tinkles like bells but is muted, more measured. Several of her bridesmaids of four years ago are now moms, and Lydia dotes on their children, not planning to have any of her own. At home, she cradles Nala in her arms, fusses over what she eats, and checks for ticks after a walk. Jake, too, cuddles with Nala after work, napping on the sofa while Lydia snaps photos of Nala snoring on Jake's belly, four legs sticking straight up into the air, and sends them to Dan and me. Walking in the park with Lydia, Jake, and Nala, as we did earlier this fine Thanksgiving Day, I watch them operate as a team: leash, harness, doggie water bottle, plastic bags for poop. A family of three.

Now, I call everyone to dinner, handing each guest a plate to help themselves at the buffet and stove. Lydia takes Nala out the front door for a last-minute pee, and suddenly I hear screaming. Through the living room window, I see copious blood. Our guests run outside and bend over Nala on our front walk. Jake, on his cell phone, is calling animal emergency rooms. A neighbor's pit bull had broken free from its leash and mauled Nala in the face, right around her eye. Lydia is crying inconsolably. Even as he agrees to cover the veterinary expenses, the neighbor is screaming at Lydia for "walking her dog in a strange neighborhood." I hear my brother Andy's girlfriend Faith, watching from the living room, say, "Everyone is in fight-flight mode right now."

Lydia and Jake bundle Nala into their car and drive off to the animal ER. John goes outside to ask the neighbor for his phone number. The neighbor begs John not to report his dog. "You're not an attorney, are you?" the neighbor asks. "College professor," John says, trying to smile.

Back in the house, the mood is somber. People are shaking their heads. Andy tries to reassure everyone that Nala will be okay, but we don't know. I look at the food cooling on the buffet table. I'm starting to get that this-can't-be-happening feeling. I remember the day Herb knew with certainty that he was dying. I had locked myself in the powder room, looked in the mirror, and said three times, *No, this is not happening.* Again, I am thinking, *No, this is not happening.* Then I look over at John, my unexpected gift, a second remarkable man so late in life, and I think, *The worst things in life can happen, and still there is another chance.*

Our guests fill their plates and wine glasses, taking their seats around the table, as Lydia's and Jake's seats remain empty, a looming absence. I cover all the serving platters with foil and try to stuff them into my one oven to keep them warm. Jake's brisket is overcooking in the crock pot. It will be hours before the kids return—shaken, exhausted, and hungry—but Nala will not lose her eye.

It is then, when I see Lydia pale-faced after her ordeal, that I realize I have cooked this whole dinner for her. Herb is gone; my mother, with her turkey baster, in her blue-and-white striped apron, is gone; and Lydia is not tinkling with laughter. Had she joined the family at the outset, for this *her* favorite dinner of the year, she would have gone around the table asking everyone what they were thankful for, a question she owns in her joyful, animal-loving heart, just like my brother Larry owns carving the turkey with his heart surgeon's hands; and I own the pleasure of cooking for others.

I sit with Lydia and Jake and their warmed-over food. The rest of the family nibbles on apple, cherry, and pumpkin pie. Jake is silent, picking at his now burnt smoked brisket; Lydia talks about the mobbed waiting room in the animal ER, other pet owners also hysterical with animal emergencies on this Thanksgiving holiday. "I expect that vets are used to managing distraught pet owners," I say. "Like Lydia," Jake says quietly, chewing. Our eyes meet momentarily. My heart swells with gratitude for this son-in-law who gets my daughter so completely.

Who are these men who understand us women so deeply they give us ballast against our own most turbulent moments? Lydia's steady, unflappable Jake. Herb, the "great tree" that fell. And now John, who says I bring him more happiness than he's ever known, which grounds and soothes me even more than cooking the perfect meal.

I think of the *Bhagavad Gita* from my yoga teacher training days—the injunction to let go of outcomes. I sniff the air. Turkey bones are simmering in my stock pot this morning after Thanksgiving. I lift the lid, peer inside, and find liquid gold: all the love I threw into planning and cooking what would be this last Thanksgiving dinner in our home, this transformation by knife, heat, and turkey baster.

With No Forethought of Grief

"Pre-planning," the funeral homes call it. "Get your affairs in order now while you can," they say. "Spare your loved ones the stress."

Man plans and God laughs, Herb often said, usually in Yiddish, as if prefiguring his own fate and, in fact, all our fates. From the time I once planned a grilled cheese luncheon for my seven-year-old friends, I was a planner. We are all planners: John wakes up in the middle of the night to choose his outfit for tomorrow; he is always thinking about his next publication. Do we imagine we can control the inevitable outcome of our lives if only we plan enough?

John, this man who is never bored, seems to have no forethought of grief. *The valiant never taste of death but once*, he says. I, on the other hand, can't think of anything else. That tomorrow is promised to no one. The futility of planning slays me. Then, I double down and plan more. When John plans, it is for something pleasurable, like our next trip; he says the real fun is the anticipation. I can be joyful, too, especially if I'm planning a party. I can do so much more than grilled cheese now.

It is our first winter in Newtown, and John has come down with Covid just in time for his seventy-ninth birthday. For some reason, I'm still testing negative, wiping down every surface in our house with Clorox and sleeping in our guest room. Sitting as far away as I possibly can at our kitchen table, I say as John finishes his avocado toast, "Let's plan a party for your eightieth birthday. Is it okay if we wait until June and hold it out of doors? I wouldn't want to host a super spreader." John shivers and coughs and blows his nose. Then he begins rattling off names. I grab pen and paper and try to keep up as his mental Rolodex revs up. Friends from Golden High School, Swarthmore, Syracuse, and Stanford. The Santa Fe, Boulder, and Bloomington friends. The tennis buddies, the skiing buddies. Former students and colleagues, cousins in Texas, Florida, Washington, D.C., and his sister in Massachusetts. Lifelong friends of his children and friends from the Trinity Church Boy Choir. New friends from my synagogue with whom, since Covid, we gather each morning on Zoom, my family too.

"Whoa," I say, laughing, "we're up to a hundred and eighty names." *They couldn't possibly all come.* I have no idea and will not know until the RSVPs flood my inbox how beloved this man is. I think about the two hundred people who showed up for Herb's funeral.

"Bagpipes," John says. "I know a piper."

"Why don't you wear the full Scottish regalia?" I say, half kidding. "I'll buy you the whole outfit for your birthday."

"You know," he says, "you are indulging my longest-held fantasy."

"Why don't we endow a scholarship at the college in honor of your birthday?" I say, now serious, "and invite your guests to donate in lieu of gifts?" We have no idea how generous our guests will be until the gifts, accolades, and well-wishes come pouring in.

Happiness cures his Covid. I realize this party is going to be the climax of his life, a celebratory summation. The planning, the joy of it, warms us both throughout the chilly winter months. "No one has ever organized such a loving, elaborate celebration for me," he says. "Thank you." My humble, grateful professor so fond of tweeds, plaids, and knits with elbow patches.

John begins researching tartan kilts online, his fantasy costume. He calls the development director at the college to set up his Health Communication student travel scholarship, writes a mission statement, and sends photos of himself with his students in South Africa and all over the world. He lists his publications and achievements and then writes, "but my greatest joy is seeing my students flourish." Anyone who knows John knows this to be true.

I open Excel and set up the "birthday spreadsheet" to track RSVPs. I get busy creating the online save-the-date message with a photo gallery of John through the ages—as a little boy, as a hippie in the anti-war movement, as a buttoned-down president of a national opinion research subsidiary in New York City, as a young father of two boys, as a mature professor grinning at the camera flanked by his thirty-something sons. Same eyes, same smile, same thick curly hair. The *tres amigos*, John says.

I design a printed invitation on Shutterfly using John's all-time favorite photo, taken out west near his parents' home. He holds and hugs his two young sons on a precipice under the vast pink-and-blue Colorado sky illuminating the snow-capped peaks of the Continental Divide behind them. I fuss over fonts and layout, and the pleasure of this work absorbs me utterly. In spite of myself, I forget my own forethought of grief. Planning can do that.

RSVPs for John's party come in each day. "I can't believe," John says, "how many people are coming to our wedding."

"Wedding?"

Our eyes meet. Long pause.

"I mean birthday party."

Why am I holding my breath? His eyes change color. Mine must have, too. *How can I stand in the way of the one thing John wants more than anything?*

"We could keep it a secret and then surprise everyone at the party with a ceremony," I say, not believing my own words, watching his face, knowing that all the pleasure emanating from those crinkled eyes is because I just said yes to his Freudian-slip proposal. In this moment, I let go of a resistance I had not yet faced because I never acknowledged it, didn't know it was there. But to be able to bring joy to another? It's probably why we parents spoil our children. *We just want her to be happy*, all those mothers and fathers said to me in the Admissions Office.

Wrong again. I still think I am agreeing to marriage only to please John, like an indulgent parent. For so long, I was certain I did not *need* to be married to him. I already felt like his wife, doing all the wifey things. My excuses, such as not needing to own property, which I had been telling him almost since the beginning, evaporate at this moment. Suddenly, I understand my resistance: I am afraid of betraying Herb, afraid of hurting his children as if marrying John would mean un-marrying their father. "John," I say, "can we ask one another's children for permission?" He nods. We start giggling like little kids as I relax and well up, realizing my longing to be married again has been at least as great as John's.

Birds titter on the feeders.

Permission

Christmas 2022, the last night of Chanukah, Lydia, Jake, and John's younger son, Maxwell, and wife, Jane, are coming for dinner. I have turned on every light in the house to chase away the cold, damp, darkening December gloom. I have placed candles in the menorah, the same hanukkiah Herb and I had used since our children were toddlers. I arrange sprigs of fragrant rosemary on the dining room table, my nod to Christmas. The kids arrive bearing gifts for us and one another, already behaving like affectionate stepsiblings, hugs all around. We haven't seen them since that "last Thanksgiving" dinner one month ago.

Nala is healed from her pit bull encounter, but she is left at home this time. Lydia, I notice, is graying a bit more around the temples, soft brown curls below her shoulders now, bouncing when she giggles. All the kids are smartly dressed, especially Jane and Maxwell, who share John's affinity for color and style. Their laughter fills our family room as we settle for drinks and nibbles. I have made the fresh guacamole with lime and cilantro that Jake loves. I have been frying latkes all day. The house smells like olive oil and onions.

Just before dinner, we say, "We have news."

Our kids are suddenly silent, tight-lipped, watching us warily. We each get down on our knees in front of the other's child, Maxwell on the brown velvet couch and Lydia in John's favorite green leather chair. We pause, then say in unison, "May. We. Have. Your. permission. To marry?" It is one of those time-stands-still moments as our kids hesitate, look at one another, and then erupt into smiles. Maxwell looks at Jane, who is misty-eyed. Lydia looks at Jake, implacable as ever, but I see a twinkle. The kids embrace us and each other. Permission to marry. From the people we love most in all the world.

Suddenly, Lydia gasps and glances conspiratorially at Jane, eyes dancing. "Mom! We must throw you a *bachelorette party!*"

"No!" I say emphatically, "I'm way too old for that. Besides, remember, this is a secret. No one can know." Except, of course, Dan and Christopher, John's other son, both out of town. We had tried on our petition in front of our firstborns the previous night on Zoom, minus the kneeling. Permission to marry, now from all four of our children.

How much easier it will be, I think, to plan a wedding no one is expecting. Still, there is the ceremony to prepare, vows to be written, rings to be found, a marriage license to apply for—requiring Herb's death certificate and John's divorce decree—and a meeting in New York with the federal judge (John's best friend from college) who will be our officiant.

And the outfits, God help us, the outfits. An across-the-bodice sash for me in the red-and-green Pollock tartan to match John's kilt, custom-made from fabric woven in Scotland. Brides in Scotland wear a plain, blessedly simple, long white dress under the sash, and I shall do just that—I've got an off-white gown hanging right in my closet that my mother once wore to my brother's wedding, already shortened and taken in to fit me. I have the perfect brooch to attach the sash with: Lydia bought me one of a cat peering into a goldfish bowl for Mother's Day when she was eight years old.

Formal wedding attire for the groom in Scotland, on the other hand, is another story. John chooses the Prince Charlie jacket with silver buttons, braided epaulets, and a matching vest. The pair of hose presents a bit of a conundrum—should they be black or white? John enjoys, as he does, his lengthy equivocation over colors. The *sgian dubh* (Gaelic for black knife) will insert part way into his hose, adorned with interwoven silver and a red Cairngorm stone decorating the top of the hilt. It will take him months to decide on his sporran, the purse a Scottish man carries on a chain around his waist, hanging near the groin. John will choose white fur, rabbit, I think. When the outfit arrives in May, it is stunning. Am I really marrying an eighty-year-old man in a skirt?

He asks if we can be Mr. and Mrs. Pollock. "Please don't ask me to change my name," I plead. "I've been Peggy Mandell for fifty years, a name I share with Herb's children." To humor John, I try on "Peggy Pollock" one evening at a restaurant, even though it will not be my legal name.

"It makes my heart soar to hear you say Peggy Pollock," John says, eyes crinkling.

Wrong again: I, too, love the alliterative ping. I love the *idea* of Peggy Pollock. I belong to John now. But I will honor Herb and all that we had, carrying Mandell with me to the grave.

With Forethought
of Grief

He could only speak out of the left side of his mouth, the right side drooping into a permanent frown. "I pushed the call button ten times to ask for a bedpan," he said, lisping, "and when the nurse came, it was too late. He called me a dirty man and beat me for messing up my sheets. I was so ashamed."

We were in our thirties when Herb's father had a massive stroke, leaving him paralyzed on the right side of his body. Admitted to the only nursing home that accepted Medicaid, he languished there, wheelchair bound, right arm atrophied, fingers curled into a claw that would not open no matter how many times Herb rubbed and stroked his hand during our weekly visits to the Hebrew Home of Greater Washington.

A corpulent, garrulous man who loved his cigars, good food, and writing pointedly impassioned letters to *The Jewish Exponent*, Morton Mandell called himself "opinionated but loveable." He never planned anything. He lived in the moment for the pleasure of striking up unhurried conversations with complete strangers who found him charming. "Come on, Morton, let's go," Herb's mother, Ethel, would say, rolling her eyes. Often out of work, Morton relied upon Ethel to make ends meet, and she had just left for work the morning Morton suffered his massive stroke. On her feet for eight hours a day, checking out groceries at the local Cash 'N Carry, she arrived home, as always, after 5 p.m. that day, ready to put her feet up, to find Morton on the dining room floor, under the wall-mounted phone, helplessly reaching just inches away. He had been lying for eight hours on the now useless right side of his body, arteries on the left side of his brain having hemorrhaged beyond repair. He would die just after his seventieth birthday.

From that day forward, Herb's determination not to suffer his father's fate became a daily preoccupation. In his forties, Herb began purchasing long-term health insurance for both of us. But there would be no long-term for him. This God who laughs while man plans had something else in mind for Herb, who would not die penniless like his father, not endure a massive stroke, and never enter a nursing home.

Here I am, wondering: how do two lovers in the autumn of their lives, clinging to one another against the ravages of old age, plan their future? How, indeed, does one exit this good earth without being beaten by a disgruntled nurse?

John understood, he said, from the moment we met, that I expected him to drop dead at any moment "because of Herb." I laughed nervously when he said that, but I also felt relief because naming a truth can take away its power. I did not yet realize that John, too, believed I could up and leave him at any time because his second wife did. Now I know that this fierce attachment on both our parts is a bulwark against the worst thing that can happen—abandonment, either willful or the result of a cruel death by suffocation. A bulwark against the disease of loneliness.

I had begun researching nursing homes when my mother was still alive. After we visited her sister-in-law (my Aunt Judy) at her Continuing Care Retirement Center, Mom said in the car ride home, "If I ever have to go into *one of those places*, please shoot me." My mother lived out her days blissfully alone in her home, content and in control. For years, she had advocated for physician-assisted suicide, joined the Hemlock Society, supported Death with Dignity, and re-written her advanced directives so many times I had file folders full of her multiple versions. All for naught, as she slipped away in the middle of the night at Chestnut Hill Hospital, leaving her last Tastykake lemon pie half-eaten on her tray table. I imagine God had a chuckle.

My plans are different. I like the idea of being around people. I like the idea of *one of those places*. John does, too, in theory, provided he can keep teaching. He reminds me that he plans to die in the classroom because federal law has no mandatory retirement age for professors.

Shortly after I met John, I hired a lawyer to help me update my will. When the lawyer said, "You know, if you marry a guy eight years your senior, you are just going to wind up being a nurse," I thought about Herb, how walking him home was the most wrenchingly beautiful chapter in our love story. I fired the lawyer. But he scared me, and I am upping my nursing home search.

We discover Pennswood Village. One of those places that happens to be a mile down the road from our home in Newtown and a stone's throw from The College of New Jersey.

Pennswood Village. Built on eighty-two acres of Bucks County farmland, some of it preserved in perpetuity as wild-flower meadows for pollinators and birds and woods with walking trails along Neshaminy Creek. Unpretentious clusters of tidy one-, two-, and three-story residences for independent living, personal care, or skilled nursing, nestled around verdant courtyards. *It could all end right here*, I think.

We tour. We attend Pennswood's symposium on Quakerism. We meet people. "Hi, I'm Ruth," says a sturdy woman with curly white hair and twinkling blue eyes. "I'm ninety-nine. I've been here twenty-nine years. Look at me! Do you see what good care Pennswood takes of its residents? I owe my physical state, as well, to thirty years of square dancing. By the way, if you move here, I will help you register to vote. Everybody here votes. You *must* vote." *Ruth was seventy when she came to Pennswood, younger than I am now.*

We meet Verena, a Swiss-born retired petrochemical engineer, and her dog, Lexi, in the gazebo by the Community Gardens, which Verena oversees. She shows us her rhubarb, raspberries, radishes, and watermelon. "Everything here is done by the residents," she says.

"This is a commune," I say to John. "It's Swarthmore College without the exams," John replies. He is starting to get that we'll-put-the-bird-feeder-over-here look on his face. That smile. I see us living here.

Soon, walking over to the gazebo at Pennswood by way of George School's equestrian center becomes our Sunday morning ritual. "The horses remind me of growing up in Colorado," John says. That smile again. Frisky chestnuts, all-white geldings, black mares, and bays with gleaming curry-combed coats and braided manes frolic in the paddock adjacent to Pennswood. We take note of the "intergenerational walkway" linking the Pennswood and George School campuses. John thinks someday, *if* he retires, he might volunteer to teach at this elite Quaker boarding school. "I could help students improve their writing skills, help them prepare for college." Maybe George School needs a yoga teacher.

We meet Gladys and her husband. "We looked at twenty-five CCRCs all over the East Coast," she says. "We chose Pennswood for its end-of-life care. There is genuine kindness among the staff," she adds. "We feel truly cared for here." I think of Morton Mandell lying on the floor for eight hours, reaching for the phone. I think of my mother and her pursuit of death with dignity.

We meet Cathy and Ben, relative newcomers to Pennswood. Ben is a former curator who worked for the National Park Service at Harper's Ferry, West Virginia. "I am an introvert," he says, "but I haven't talked as much as I have here. People are just so friendly." Cathy chimes in with a big smile: "I haven't laughed or played so much in a long time, especially in the weekly volleyball game." She shares her notes from today's

Science Times discussion group. "I look forward to those discussions with brilliant retired scientists every week."

We meet Steve, head of the Pennswood Birders, and his wife, Deidre, a retired professor of Africana Studies and co-founder of Pennswood's Parkinson's support group. Together, they attend La Mesa Española (the Spanish table) for people—like John—who love practicing their conversational Spanish. We meet Larry, a tenor in the Princeton Pro Musica, who is helping to found a chorale at Pennswood. How I long to find a local choir to join; the commute to my old synagogue choir in Fort Washington has become untenable.

Each time we visit, we look around at these genteel, stylishly dressed residents—a former judge, a college president, a landscape architect, professors, surgeons, scientists, clergy, and CEOs in their eighties and nineties who want us to know there is no better place than Pennswood, how grateful they are to be there. At Pennswood, you don't die, they say; you graduate. We notice how intently curious they are about us, and suddenly, we realize *we* are being vetted by *them*. "This is like joining a fraternity," John says. "It's like college admissions," I say. We have no idea yet how true that is. Until the cognitive assessment, the SAT of senior living. We add our names to the five-year waiting list and continue to settle in at Randolph Court. John replenishes the bird feeders.

During our first summer at Randolph Court, John is scrambling to empty and sell his Princeton home while the post-Covid sellers' market is still hot. One day, I receive an unexpected phone call from Mark and Laura, our landlords. So sorry, they say, but they need to move back into their home as soon as our lease is up. Practically in tears, John says, "I'm not ready to move all over again." I had already moved twice since Herb died and sold and emptied my mother's house, my few remnants of Herb's art collection, paintings from my mom, and framed family photos still in boxes so John could "have the walls." We had successfully merged John's artwork and my furniture. We are nesting, throwing small dinner parties for John's friends and mine. We are planning to host a real Thanksgiving dinner. We are expecting to stay for at least four years. Pennswood is supposed to be *one of those places* "down the road." John buys suet for the bird feeder.

The next day, a postcard arrives in the mail. I recognize the distinctive, classy, but understated Pennswood Village logo, a tree inside a medallion, and lettering embossed in gold. *Announcing immediate construction of "The Meadows," thirty new independent living apartments! As priority waitlist members, you are invited to our exclusive preview reception ...*

At the reception, there are architectural renderings, floor plans, and specs with square footage for three different models. There is filet mignon, jumbo shrimp, cannolis, wine, and live harp music. And our very own tote bag with a postcard to sign, committing us to reserve an apartment before they announce it to the public—a two-week deadline. *Two weeks?*

We must leave Randolph Court. We know we love Pennswood. And with a shrug, we sign.

Is God laughing *with* us?

But first, the dreaded cognitive assessment. No swimsuit contest, but complete financial disclosure since we will be paying Pennswood for the rest of our lives. No swimsuit contest, but a test of short-term memory: repeating back five unrelated words after several minutes' delay (I struggle, John aces it). Replicating geometric shapes to demonstrate spatial awareness. Our medical history is reviewed. We pass. We are given day privileges for the rest of the year during the construction of our new home. John joins La Mesa Española with Steve and Deidre. I submit an excerpt from my memoir to *Village Voices*, the resident-run literary magazine. John takes note of the many shelves in the Pennswood Village library devoted to "Pennswood authors" and imagines his books there, maybe someday a memoir by Margaret Mandell. I practice yoga and swim, joking with the women in the locker room about growing older, laughing at our uncooperative bodies, our thinning hair, and the traffic jam of walkers and mobility devices blocking the lockers. We lift weights and take aerobic dance with Brian, a wildly popular former Riverdance performer who teaches "Silver Strong" and keeps us laughing. John bravely auditions to sing bass in the Pennswood Chorale, having not sung since his freshman year in college. I quit my synagogue choir. We begin rehearsing weekly at Pennswood and every night in our kitchen with a borrowed electronic keyboard. We perform in the spring concert, some of the most demanding choral repertoire I have ever sung. I ask them to list me as "Peggy Pollock" in the program notes. We will not die with the music still inside of us.

Who are these people with whom we will spend the rest of our lives? They are just like us: scared, vulnerable, grateful to be engaged in challenging, purposeful work, and above all, not to be alone. People who embrace the Quaker values of service, simplicity, and stewardship of the environment. People who eschew organ recitals and senseless complaining about old age because they would rather laugh and give thanks for today. Their kindness is palpable.

The idea of Pennswood is one of *return*, I think. For me, it feels like returning to Springside, my childhood prep school and employer for twenty years. Don't we all long to return to something familiar at the end of our days, an antidote to the terror of embarking upon the truly unknown? What is planning if it isn't finding kindred spirits, fellow travelers on the last leg of life's journey with the finish line in view?

We have vetted and been vetted by an entire community. We can't wait to be part of it. After the wedding, we think, we will be on a permanent honeymoon at Pennswood Village.

Because we planned.

More Time

"I fell in love with you one paragraph at a time," John says beneath the white *brise-soleil* pergola festooned with roses. The sapphire sky cloudless, rendering the light both resplendent and dappled through the surrounding trees. Cool breezes luffing his tartan kilt, the silver buttons on his Prince Charlie jacket sparkling in the sun.

"I pledge myself to you, John Crothers Pollock III, you who have loved me back to life," I answer, tartan sash draped across my chest from right shoulder to left hip, having just processed down the aisle with Dan.

Ninety-nine unsuspecting guests had been instructed to gather in front of the pergola, not knowing why, mouths agape, bellies full of cinnamon French toast and chicken marsala.

This eightieth birthday brunch turned flash mob wedding is, for John and me, the stuff of dreams we didn't know we had. I had forgotten my little girl "here comes the bride" fantasy, nurtured since I first saw a picture of my mother at age eighteen in her 1947 Nan Duskin wedding dress. No guests came to my first wedding with Herb in 1974. My father, in the middle of a bitter divorce, had refused to walk me down the aisle with my mother and told me he could not afford to pay for a wedding and give us a gift, too. We chose the gift, not understanding the role of witnesses in the sanctification of a union. It would be many decades before I realized that just as funerals are not for the deceased but for those we leave behind, so too weddings are for those who bear witness: the bride and groom cannot be an "us" without the blessing of community. And what a community has shown up for John's birthday!

The procession is an afterthought. The week before, I had texted Dan, asking if he'd be willing to walk me down the aisle and give me away to John. An honor, Dan says. *Oh, Herb, what a gracious son we raised.*

Now I need bridesmaids, I think. *A real wedding!* I ask Lydia and John's daughter-in-law Jane to be my matrons of honor. *Wasn't I just Lydia's mother of the bride?* Dan is bringing his girlfriend, Jill, whom I'd met twice. I ask Dan's permission to email her and ask her to be a bridesmaid. "I'm in," she shoots back, "under one condition: please tell me what to wear!" Two photos appear in my inbox of Jill in two different floral print dresses and two Kentucky Derby-type hats cocked on her head, both show-stopping. I pick the pink one, to which Jill replies, "Done!"

Uh-oh. What about John's sister Mary, traveling from Marblehead, Massachusetts, who thinks she's coming to a birthday party? John insists we call her and spill the beans so we can invite her to join the wedding party. Mary arrives in a white linen cocktail-length dress, high-heeled sandals, and a classic straw hat. My beautiful bridesmaids, so willing, so game, so thrilled to be in on the surprise. Lydia in her floor-length floral print, "garden party chic" she calls it, all sweetness and light; Maxwell's Jane with her evanescent smile and bright red dress to complement Maxwell's forest-green suit, both matching John's red-and-green Pollock tartan.

At the appointed time, the girls and Dan and I assemble at the opposite end of the garden as Jed, our officiant, dons his black judge's robe and John joins him under the pergola, flanked on his left by his "groomsmen"—son Maxwell, Lydia's husband Jake, and Mary's partner, Tom, in his own tartan sash.

Ninety-nine guests wait and watch. Maxwell starts to play Skye Boat Song through our sound system as Lydia and

Jane walk solemnly in step towards the pergola. Then, elegant Mary and whimsical, long-legged Jill, who has changed her mind about the hat and is now sporting a wreath of flowers in her hair to match her dress, a forest nymph. As the ladies arrange themselves under the pergola to John's right, I slip my arm into Dan's, and we process, my eyes riveted on John, his on me. Passing through the gauntlet of bystanders, our astonished guests begin to cheer as one guest calls out, "John, did you know about this?" Silence again as our officiant begins the ceremony, inviting John and me to share our vows. I have mostly memorized what I wrote and am able to watch John's face as I speak. His eyes are locked onto mine as if, he tells me later, at that moment, no one else is there.

"I have never felt so seen," he says.

But it is I who feels seen.

"You may kiss," Jed says as Maxwell hits the play button for "Give It to Me Baby," and the crowd erupts into rhythmic clapping. We turn towards the beaming faces around us and break into our aerobic dance sequence that we learned from our Pennswood fitness class and have been rehearsing nightly in our kitchen for the past month.

Our beloved witnesses. John's former students, now wildly successful in their fields of endeavor, keep telling me that John believed in them before they believed in themselves. My brothers, Pete and Andy, who text our busy, faraway brothers, Larry and Don, with breaking news: "Your sister just got married." Our morning minyan friends from synagogue, old high school, college, graduate school, tennis, and skiing buddies of John's. Four of my first cousins and my dear Aunt Judy, old friends of mine, including one I've known since childhood who took me to his senior prom: "John," he says as the party ends, "you're a lucky guy."

Our beloved witnesses. They *know*, as John says in his vows, quoting from the Bhagavad Gita, that we are meant to "intervene in one another's sorrow." And so, we do.

The night before the wedding, I find myself upstairs rummaging through old photographs and discovering a slightly blurry Kodak Instamatic 8 X 10 blow-up of Herb and me standing by a small cake at the Blue Bell Inn where our immediate families had gathered for dinner following a ceremony witnessed only by my four brothers and Herb's three siblings. No wedding gown for me, a tan polyester suit for Herb. We are smiling broadly, I striking a silly pose as I often did as a twenty-three-year-old, not yet chastened by life. Next, I unearth a manilla envelope labeled "*Ketubah*," the Jewish marriage contract Herb and I signed before a rabbi on June 8, 1974, written in Hebrew and English. I bring it downstairs to John: "Do you know what this is?" I ask. "Have you ever seen one of these before?" He nods, then is silent. I quickly take the *Ketubah* away, walk back upstairs, blow one last kiss to my twenty-four-year-old groom in the tan polyester suit, and return to John with a prenuptial hug, kissing his white sideburns and bushy eyebrows.

For the entire week following the wedding, photos and videos keep showing up on Facebook, and the news of our surprise wedding spreads. I am warmed by the outpouring of congratulations from former work colleagues, Springside alumnae, far-flung relatives, and even yoga-teacher-training classmates from Kripalu. I am not prepared for one fulsome response from a woman whom I met six years ago at my first Tulum, Mexico yoga and writing retreat the year after Herb died, just months after abdominal surgery. I had traveled alone and arrived knowing no one, the scar on my belly still itching and pulling apart during downward facing dog, my mind still in a fog of grief. One night, she sat with me at dinner, and I told her about losing Herb. I did not yet know that her husband, also a physician, had been recently diagnosed with leukemia. "How do you manage?" she asked. "I don't know if I could be as brave as you." Six years later, her husband still in remission, she sees my wedding video on Facebook and writes,

"I am so happy that you have found love. You were so brave about being alone." *Am I brave?* After finding John, I could barely remember the soul-crushing loneliness I felt on that first trip to Tulum. *Yes, I am brave.* My mother had the courage, she said just before she died, to leave Dad. I have the courage to trust love one more time.

In the weeks leading up to the wedding, I notice, as never before, how at least once a day and sometimes several times a day, John makes an observation or connection, ponders a question I have never considered, drawing upon a lifetime of reading, study, scholarship, and unquenchable curiosity. A day has not gone by, I realize, in which I do not see the world differently, learn something new, just sitting with John at the kitchen table reading *The New York Times* or watching PBS News Hour. I rejoice. *This is how the rest of our days together are going to be!* Now, I greet him each morning with our customary bear hug but also new excitement—*what will we talk about today?*

Two days after our wedding, I am standing at the kitchen sink washing dishes. I feel John's warm breath on the back of my neck, his hand on my shoulder.

"It feels so good," he whispers into my hair, then hesitates, choking back a sob, "it feels so good to be married."

I turn and hold him, stroking his tear-stained cheeks.

"I don't think I've ever admitted to myself until just now," he says, "I've been so lonely for so, so long."

Now you will not know the cold, for you will each be warmth to the other.
Now you will not know the dark, for you will each be light to the other.
Now you have raised a shelter against the loneliness of human existence.

Jed had read these words from the Navajo wedding blessing as we stood under the pergola in the presence of loved ones, once strangers to one another, now bound together as witnesses.

I see you, John. I am yours. Let us be brave for one another.

EPILOGUE

My Dearest Love, Herb:

Forty-nine years ago today, we placed gold rings on one another's fingers, clueless about the future yet expecting great goodness from life. Seven-and-a-half years ago, just before you departed this earth, you told me your life had been so much better than you ever could have imagined. Of all the cherished moments we shared, I cling to that one—your prayer of gratitude for a good life as you faced its end.

My prayer was different and still is. A prayer of supplication, which I uttered for the first time during our last summer on Prince Edward Island, not knowing yet somehow knowing we would never return. I discovered this prayer at the end of a journal entry written at dawn that summer:

Sunrise. The sun sits just above the top of an evergreen tree across the bay, as if the tree gave birth to it. Clouds have moved across that shimmering orb, creating a warm, pink glow. The air is soft and still. Seagulls call to one another. Otherwise, silence. At dinner last night, Herb lit a candle and placed it between us. He put on the CD of Samuel Barber's Adagio for Strings. We sat down to a cheese omelet with fresh basil from our neighbor's garden and a side of zucchini cooked in garlic and olive oil tossed with steamed PEI potatoes. Herb said, "This was the most fantastic day."

While Herb was at the library yesterday, I started missing him and wondered if I would ever be capable of living alone. When he came home with Motown CDs, and I started dancing in the kitchen, it wasn't just the music; it was the happiness of looking across the room and seeing him there. How could we sixty-somethings be that much in love? More in love than at any other time in our lives, perhaps because of all our years together, perhaps because of our heightened awareness that all this is going to end. Please, not yet, please not yet.

After you died, after the worst thing that could happen happened, I continued to plead for more time and still do. Perhaps the God who laughs while man plans has a little something more in mind for me before I take my leave. A little more joy, a few more laughs, a tad more wisdom so hard won in dark times, another chance to love fiercely.

Four days ago, I married John and placed one of our gold rings, resized, on his left hand. He will never take it off, he says, still believing he is the beneficiary of the deep love I felt for you and poured into fourteen books of letters after you died, many of which he's heard me read aloud. From the day we met, John understood I was writing to heal, to write my way through grief and loss. Somehow, he knew that he could be my witness. John intervened in my sorrow, as he wrote in his wedding vows, as I intervened in his, giving each of us a last chance at love in this, our home stretch.

Yes, it all ends, but not yet, I pray, not yet.

Here I am, once again, speaking to you as if ashes can hear. Because I want you to know I did it, baby, as you foretold, found a new special someone and hitched my wagon to his! I know you would have liked John—his innate goodness, his decency, his great dancing. I know you didn't really send him to me. I found him all by myself and then set about the task of knowing him, caring for him, and continuing on the path of becoming my best self in the presence of another, as you and I did for the time we were given.

After you died, I had no idea how to be in the world and did a lot of pretending, acting, and looking like myself, like the mighty gum tree in our backyard whose bark gave the appearance of solidity but was completely hollow on the inside, about to topple and crumble, becoming one with the earth as you are now, and as I shall be but *not yet, please not yet.*

You are not listening—you are not here. And yet, at our wedding four days ago, Dan danced with me to a Motown song and snapped his fingers exactly like you. Lydia was my magnificent matron of honor. You are not listening, but I am still listening to you, holding your prayer of gratitude for life's great gifts in my heart, including the gift of finding John.

I think you would like the person I've become, a whole tree again inside and out, standing tall, for now.

And Always
One More Time

Acknowledgments

In grade school, I was always the shortest one in my class. Now, I stand on the shoulders of giants. Two of them are my first-ever writing coaches, twenty years my junior, and twice as wise. Intuitive, loving, and demanding, they each took a chance on me, a neophyte, knowing exactly when and how to push and prod, when to affirm and encourage.

There would be no book without my first writing teacher, Jennifer Schelter, who heard me read one of my letters written to Herb shortly after he died. She took me aside after class and said, "There is such a love story here. This must become a book." A thousand letters later, during the Covid pandemic, I called Jennifer and asked her, if I transcribed my letters into a manuscript, would she be my first reader? Her gracious and resounding "yes" came with reading assignments: several riveting memoirs to learn the genre and an iconic textbook, *Handling the Truth* by Beth Kephart, a renowned memoirist and teacher of the craft.

For nineteen months, Jennifer and I slogged our way through my letters, through tears and laughter, tightening, shortening, exercising the "brevity muscle," rewriting scenes and dialogue, playing with "dummy fixes" and "beat sheets." Half movie director, half watercolorist, Jennifer compelled me to render my story with brush strokes, trusting the reader to fill in the white space. Pages of commentary and analysis gave way to emotional color. "Where's the yearning?" she asked on every page. "What does this feel like in your body?" "Where's the white, hot center?" "Where's the turn?" "Where's the conflict?" "Trouble is your friend."

I faced many demons, bristling and resisting when it became too hard, too raw, too true. Jennifer stayed with me, especially when I pushed back. Steady, compassionate, unrelenting. Just what I needed.

I reread *Handling the Truth* by Beth Kephart, saw how far I had come, and understood I had so much still to learn. I reached out to Beth, sharing pieces of my writing with her. By some miracle, Beth took me on as a student, and we went to work. Beth divined immediately that my writing only letters was confining me. Lost in the weeds of revision, I was unsure of the arc of my story. "Step away from the book," she said. "Write me four pieces. One, what is your emotional core? Two, what is your hierarchy of themes? Rank order them. Three, what is your back flap copy for the book? Four, what would a critic write about your book in *The New York Times Book Review*?"

Meanwhile, Beth took one of my chapters and sorted it into letters and not-letters, and more were not-letters! "Do you see the difference?" she asked. I excavated the entire book, discovering more not-letters than letters, which released me from the constraint of the epistolary form into the deeper realm of creative storytelling, turning letters into chapters. "Go big, go deep, go wide," she said, seeing what wasn't on the page as well as what was, like Michelangelo seeing the David still imprisoned in the stone. "Now write just about yourself, who you are apart from the men in your life." First, I recoiled, shrank, having forgotten who I had been, was still in the midst of becoming: the essential me. The more I wrote, the taller I felt; stature conferred by writing, a reclamation of self. Then she asked for new chapters, new letters as I began to acquire the subtle grace of tonal shift from letter to story and back. "More is needed here," she said. "I am pushing you harder than I have ever pushed anyone because I know it's there." Floodgates opened, and the story enlarged, universalized.

How did she know?

There would be no *And Always One More Time* but for Beth Kephart.

I stand on the shoulders of giants.

Every editor I've encountered along the way had something important to teach me. Andrea Firth and Dinty W. Moore at *Brevity Blog*; Jeannie Ralston at *NextTribe*; Sari Botton at *Oldster Magazine*; Michelle Redo, host of the *Daring to Tell* podcast; the intrepid editorial team at Atmosphere Press, Gracie Meadows, Alex Kale, Tammy Letherer, and the unsung heroes of proofreading, all midwives to my completed book; and Atmosphere's gifted cover designer, Felipe Betim, who spins thoughts into gold.

Perhaps the bravest of all were my early readers of the manuscript, beginning with my patient, magnanimous children, Dan and Lydia Mandell, for whom my stories evoked painful as well as happy memories. So too, my new stepson, Maxwell Pollock, who escorted me into the digital marketing world with his brilliant website design. My equally generous brothers, Larry, Andy, Pete, and Don Klein; my sisters-in-law, Diane Horowitz, Ph.D., Kate Klein, and Anna-Maria Klein; and my mother, Bobbie Klein, who listened through tears of equanimity and kindness when I read aloud at family gatherings. As well, my first cousins, Ellen and Harvey Ussery, and Sally and Rabbi Michael Klein-Katz, paragons of empathy and wisdom. My spiritual guides, Rabbis Vivian Schirn, Joshua Waxman, Ph.D., and Alanna Sklover, each a shining presence in my most vulnerable moments. Many dear friends, both longtime and recent, including Ruth and Jules Mermelstein, Esq., Priscilla Sands, Ed.D., Karen Tracy, Sondra Saull, M.D., Hildy Armour, Edith Newhall, Kay Franklin, Esq., Lindsey Lang, Esq., Sandra Evans, Ellen Reath, Esq., Daniel Schwarz, Ph.D., Kathy Schoengold, Laura Todd, Ann Rakoff, Ed.D., Jess Frey, Anne Baber, and Phyllis Purscell. I have treasured their thoughtful, incisive feedback. I am the better for it.

For many, writing is a solitary, lonely business. Never for

me. Two muses, one living, one dead, never left my side from the very first letter to the epilogue. Herb Mandell dwells forever in my head and heart, an inspiration and life-long companion in his presence and his absence. John Pollock became almost instantly not only my muse and confidante but an editor of such extraordinary acumen that I dared not send my work out into the world before it passed through the portal of his discerning ear and always one more time. My muses, my loves.

About Atmosphere Press

Founded in 2015, Atmosphere Press was built on the principles of Honesty, Transparency, Professionalism, Kindness, and Making Your Book Awesome. As an ethical and author-friendly hybrid press, we stay true to that founding mission today.

If you're a reader, enter our giveaway for a free book here:

SCAN TO ENTER
BOOK GIVEAWAY

If you're a writer, submit your manuscript for consideration here:

SCAN TO SUBMIT
MANUSCRIPT

And always feel free to visit Atmosphere Press and our authors online at atmospherepress.com. See you there soon!

About the Author

Photo credit: Karen Tracy

Darwin once wrote survival of the fittest means survival of the most adaptable. **MARGARET MANDELL**'s life story is one of adaptation to changing circumstances. She has been a college teacher and doctoral candidate, a mother of two, an entrepreneur, an independent school admissions director, a triathlete, and a certified yoga instructor. When her husband of many years passed away, she became a widow, a woman still in the midst of becoming. Her debut memoir, *And Always One More Time*, tells the story of her next act and new, sustaining love. Excerpts have appeared in *The Metaworker Literary Magazine*, *Brevity Blog*, *NextTribe*, *Oldster Magazine*, and the *Daring to Tell* podcast.

www.ingramcontent.com/pod-product-compliance
Lightning Source LLC
Chambersburg PA
CBHW021407150726
47989CB00005B/2445